DEF LEPPARD

TWO STEPS AHEAD

DEF LEPPARD

TWO STEPS AHEAD

Dave Bowler and Bryan Dray

B✧**XTREE**

Published in Great Britain in 1996 by
Boxtree Limited,
Broadwall House, 21 Broadwall, London SE1 9PL.

© 1996 Dave Bowler and Bryan Dray

Front cover design: Shoot That Tiger!

Front cover photos: Retna

Typeset by SX Composing DTP, Rayleigh, Essex
Printed by The Bath Press, Bath

ISBN 0 7522 2241 4

10 9 8 7 6 5 4 3 2 1

A CIP catalogue is available from
the British Library.

CONTENTS

DEDICATION

To Mom and Dad
'Bicycles, muscles, cigarettes' – Raymond Carver
And for Denise
The half moon in the sky tonight, bright enough to come up with
an answer . . .
Always

David

To Trish, Emma and Rebecca
For all their love and support.
And Mum, Dad, Gran, Joyce and Wal
For all their help.

Bryan

ACKNOWLEDGEMENTS

It wouldn't be possible to put together any book without the help of a number of people. Paramount among these are Clare Hulton at Boxtree and Tanja Howarth and Mark Hayward who continue to take care of business. We are grateful to them all.

Much of the initial basic research was conducted at the National Sound Archive, an excellent facility. We are very grateful to all the staff there who were unfailingly helpful and able to suggest numerous avenues of enquiry. Thanks too to those at the Colindale Newspaper Library. Above all, we are most grateful to Denise Dean who, as usual, gave far too much time to the research of this project, as well as offering thoughts on the text.

Thanks too are due to the very legendary *Hot Press, Q, Select, Vox, New Musical Express, Kerrang!, Melody Maker, Raw, Metal Hammer* and *Record Mirror* whose articles on the band were an excellent source of information.

Without the help of 'Anthology 2' from the Beatles, sanity would have passed away much sooner than it did. The same applies to Maria McKee's 'Life Is Sweet' and the Cowboy Junkies' '200 More Miles'. No collection is complete without them.

Finally, if there's anyone on the lookout for other Def Leppard fans to share information with, you should send a large SAE to Kate at Midlands Metal International, 47 Thackeray Walk, Stafford, Staffordshire ST17 9SE.

INTRODUCTION

'We wanted to be the biggest rock band in the world.' Before embarking on the story of Def Leppard, it's important that you take notice of that single phrase. As espoused by lead singer Joe Elliott, that has long been the core philosophy of the band, their manifesto, their raison d'être. Since their formation in Sheffield some twenty years ago at the height of the punk wars, virtually every move has been made with that goal uppermost in their minds. Backed by an American management team that move with the precision of any major industrial corporation, they have unflinchingly aimed for the top and have made all the personal sacrifices necessary to get there. As Leppard's story unfolds, it becomes apparent that that bald statement of fact and of ambition has been central to their survival. You may feel it is a perfectly sensible goal. You may commend their honesty in openly confessing to the hidden agenda that motivates most groups. Alternatively you may be repelled by such naked determination to pursue relentlessly the rewards of commercialism, and be concerned that sales figures have obstructed the search for musical purity, if such a thing exists. That is your choice, but it does not change the facts. Def Leppard wanted to be big.

The reasons for dwelling on this particular point will become clear later on in this tale. Suffice it to say that these dreams lead them unerringly towards expulsion from their homeland early on in their career, victims of the vitriol of British fans at a time when the musical roost was ruled by the independent, by the DIY ethic, by the belief

1

that small was beautiful and that major label corporatism was the kiss of death for honest musical expression. Ridiculed in the early eighties by the English press, Def Leppard had to make it abroad, notably in America, before the British took them to their hearts; by the time 'Hysteria', its big rock sound and good time attitude made the airwaves in 1987, the band was finally in sync with the prevailing zeitgeist all over the 'civilised' world, including the UK. Dreams of global domination had seen them through that initial rejection and had helped them weather personal tragedy in the most dignified and courageous manner. As a consequence, some see Def Leppard as a collection of manipulative, cynical manouverers, backed up by a scheming, Machiavellian management team. Yet while no-one would pretend that they are naive idealists – such people do not exist at the top of the musical tree – single-minded determination, a quality they possess in spades, is the real secret of their success and their longevity.

If Def Leppard have been prophets without honour in their own land, then at least the profits pouring in from other lands have provided ample consolation. Joe Elliott was to boast later, with good reason, that Leppard had rewritten the rule book when it came to writing and recording rock music. Equally, they helped change British attitudes to the function of rock music and especially to commercial success. Although criticism wounded them, their determination to make it big, to make themselves 'recession proof' as Elliott termed them, enabled them to rise above the storm. Def Leppard are living proof that success can be had, enjoyed, it can be survived and it can be worth having, all ideas that were largely alien to a British perspective. Name any British band that became an international success in the seventies and you'll find a group that was instantly reviled. Queen and Genesis are excellent examples of the prevailing mindset; lauded as innovators at the outset of their careers, once they began to accumulate a few gold records, the warmth accorded them by the critics fell in direct proportion. Keen students of rock history, Leppard knew that a similar fate would inevitably await them and so simply set their faces against it and got on with the job in hand, creating mouldbreaking, classic rock music.

Of course, such a view does simplify things a little too much. Credibility, that nebulous ideal, dictates that it is almost always the dance acts, the remixers, the DJs and the avant garde industrialists who get the credit for pushing back the musical frontiers yet Leppard did as much as anyone to bring music into the digital age. Their work with Robert 'Mutt' Lange was truly groundbreaking and even such a sage as Bono remarked that 'Hysteria' was the first technological record and one that had an intellectual impact on the direction U2 took for 'Achtung Baby' and then 'Zooropa', utilizing the equipment that was at their disposal. Just as Queen had blazed a trail in their era, Def Leppard were the first band of their vintage to stretch the recording studio to its limits and to use it as another instrument, a perfectly valid response to the bewildering growth in musical technology through the 1980s.

People's suspicions about Leppard are generally roused by their management structure. So stringently are their affairs managed that the music seems to be just another division of Def Leppard Inc., a multinational moneymaking conglomerate. Music should have a romantic air about it, there should be a hint of the medieval troubadour about artists, minstrels making their merry way from town to town. Sadly, the modern world does not live on romance but on hard cash and again, Leppard were among the first to realize that harsh fact of life. They'd seen many musicians run crying to the papers to tell stories of how they'd been ripped off and they vowed it would not happen to them. More than that though, they quickly realized – and were speedily educated in the realities by manager Peter Mensch – that they could only reach the top and then stay there by giving their absolute attention to the finest of detail. Genesis were perfect examples of that and by the end of the 1970s they were one of the top acts in the world. Their blueprint was followed and built upon by Mensch and his staff to ensure that everything within the Leppard organization worked smoothly. Given their ability to attract problems, it was as well that they had such a staunch and shrewd ally as Mensch to fall back on – few other bands would have survived the hostile reception that Leppard got at Reading in 1980, the critical panning they received in the UK in the early eighties or the trials and tribulations that surrounded the making of 'Hysteria'. It was as much a tribute to Mensch's wise counsel as the innate good sense of the band that they not only survived but prospered. Good business sense can be seen as soulless, the men in suits ruling the group, but that's a gross distortion of the facts. Even if it were true, such global penetration of the Leppard sound means that everyone has a chance to hear their records and, if you're a fan of classic rock, that can only be a good thing. Def Leppard are anything but a bunch of manipulated meatheads.

Self-sufficiency is their creed and their greatest gift, crucial in the changes they are currently going through. Unlike a number of their contemporaries – notably on the west coast of America – the members of the band are down to earth blokes who can live a normal life away from the stage. It's hard to believe, but some rock musicians are so pampered that they don't know how to buy postage stamps! Def Leppard are ordinary men who have an extraordinary job. They are in touch with their fans, know that they are appreciated and are normal enough to enjoy the privileges. But above and beyond that, they are content with the music they make. That has always been the supreme test. If they make a record and love it at the end of the recording process, that is now the real success, an indication of how time has changed their attitudes. With more money in the bank than they could ever need, sales graphs are less important. Having been the *biggest* band in the world, Leppard embarked on a different road with 'Slang'. Now they want to be the *best*. 'Slang' lacks the total confidence and conviction that such a bold move requires, but it is a very encouraging first step and one that few in their position would have tried. But that is Def Leppard in a nutshell – the most self-sufficient, self-confident band in the world.

How do they justify such arrogance . . .

1

NOWHERE TO RUN?

'Def Leppard will play here in 1980.' A simple scrawl on the granite wall of Sheffield's City Hall in the bleak midwinter of 1978. An ephemeral chalk mark washed away by a rainstorm, few would have seen it at the time, yet Joe Elliott's concise statement is archetypal Def Leppard, for it reads in such a matter of fact manner that it seemed incontrovertible, defied question. In Def Leppard's case of course, the experience of the last twenty years adds immense significance to the words. Viewed that way, it does look like a statement of fact, almost a warning to the punters to book early to avoid disappointment. Such a conclusion might reasonably be dismissed as plain daft, the result of hindsight and an unquenchable desire to romanticize further the story of a major league rock band, suggesting that the hand of destiny has always been guiding Def Leppard's fortunes. After all, there are plenty of similar messages written on halls in most major towns and cities, the desperate words of an ambitious youngster looking hopelessly for a break, trying to gain extra attention for his or her group. The odd thing about it though is that Joe honestly believed that those words *were* a matter of fact, that they were a warning to get in line for tickets because he never had any doubts that his band would soon be treading the boards that had already been graced by his heroes, groups like Mott the Hoople and Thin Lizzy.

Like many kids of his age, Joe Elliott found the mid seventies dank and depressing times. Born in Sheffield on 1 August 1959, he had few academic pretensions and left school at the first opportunity, going straight out to work for a living – these were the days when Sheffield was still a thriving town and the epicentre of the world's steel industry. Jobs were plentiful and lads like Joe with no real qualifications nor ambitions for a career were thought of as ideal factory fodder. Early on he found himself working for Smith Widdowson and Eadem Limited, on the treadmill in a factory that produced cutlery, one of the city's staple products. With few prospects and the tedious grind of the nine to five stretching out before him for the next forty or fifty years, Joe was understandably filled with the desire to escape. Again, nothing there to distinguish him from thousands of others across the country, making the contemporary journey into the heart of the rat race. Joe followed the traditional escapist routes, immersing himself in pubs and football, but he always felt that there had to be more to life than just this.

Music was his greatest passion, providing a very necessary outlet for his fertile imagination. Later, he recalled that 'the first concert I ever saw was T Rex at the Sheffield City Hall in 1971. Marc Bolan was the first pop idol I ever had'. The twelve year-old was bitten by the rock'n'roll bug, those waking hours not reserved for Sheffield United being spent on dreams of pop stardom. Those formative years back in the early seventies were played out to a very strong pop soundtrack, with glam rock holding sway in the charts, courtesy of Slade, the Sweet, Gary Glitter, Roxy Music, David Bowie and Mott the Hoople. That period is often ridiculed now, largely because of the atrocious fashion sense displayed by the stars of the era, but if you can ignore the lack of anything approaching sartorial elegance and instead listen to the music, it's clear that there were some excellent songwriters and musicians around at the time. Following in the aftermath of the Beatles, whatever happened would have had to be anti-climactic but in retrospect, the power pop sensibilities of Jimmy Lea and Noddy Holder in Slade, the innovative intelligence of David Bowie, Mick Ronson, Bryan Ferry and Brian Eno and the sheer stupidity of Gary Glitter conspired to create some memorable moments.

Joe Elliott was among those moved and inspired by what was happening in the Top Twenty. 'I got off first on people like Led Zeppelin and then on the commercial side of rock – glam rock if you like, harder edged pop. Mott the Hoople were my favourite band and the good thing was that you'd get to see them and the Sweet or Slade on the TV on *Top of the Pops* but you only ever heard about Zeppelin at parties or from friends.' With typical pugnacity, Joe decided there and then that he was going to be a pop star, going so far as to inform his careers teacher of the fact. Bands like Mott had such a hold on his imagination that he created his own imaginary band, daydreaming about playing the City Hall while lessons went on around him. He even went so far as to design gig posters for this mental combo which he had named Deaf Leopard. His determination and his desire were only reinforced every time he heard 'All The Young Dudes', 'Suffragette City' or 'Blockbuster', though predictably his teachers had little faith in his ability to emulate his heroes and were not surprised when he quickly found his way on to the factory floor.

Exposure to the tedium of work only hardened Elliott's attitudes to the future. Changing jobs, he felt even less inclined to build a future for himself within a local firm. He remembered later the reason for his belief in 'Deaf Leopard'. 'I wanted to get into a band to get out of the factories. I was a storekeeper at Osborne Mushet Tools, stuck in a basement where I had to buy in everything from paper towels to Swarfega to oil rags to nuts and bolts to grinding wheels. The whole idea of being in a band was to escape boredom, so I just created my own form of escapism. When I was working, I just wanted to have a great time at night before I went to sleep and woke up to the same old crap. That's what I did for five years. I used to listen to my Alice Cooper tapes during dinner hour and think "I don't want to work here for the next fifty years. Anything to get out of this shit".'

It's a convenient phrase that we've all used countless times: 'I'd do anything to be able to pack in this job and be rich and/or famous.' Few people actually do anything about it though. They don't really mean it, don't have the courage, the conviction, the determination, the vision or the talent to do anything but dream. What set Joe Elliott apart from the rest was his intense determination to succeed and his incredible blind faith in his own ability to deliver that dream. Given that Yorkshiremen are often fairly opinionated and sure that their way is the right way, perhaps Joe's own self-assurance was just a matter of heredity – it is the county that spawned the likes of Fred

Trueman, Harvey Smith, Geoffrey Boycott and Foggy Dewhurst after all and none of them could be described as shrinking violets or lacking in self-confidence. Once he had embarked on a life in a band, the very idea of failing simply didn't occur to him. Such confidence, bordering on arrogance is remarkable when you bear in mind the enormous failure rate within the music industry. Look at any local gig guide and you can find dozens of bands of all kinds playing in the pubs and clubs of your town or city – the chances are that none of them will ever amount to anything more than just a good night out in your locale. The likelihood of any of them becoming the most successful band in the world is so infinitesimally tiny as to be not worth considering. With a band up and running, Joe turned that idea on its head so that the chances of them *not* becoming the biggest band in the world weren't worth considering.

However good or determined you are though, luck always has a part to play. Joe's particular stroke of good fortune came when he teamed up with another young man who was equally convinced of his own particular destiny. Richard Savage was a year younger than Joe, born in Sheffield on 2 December 1960. A useful guitarist, he was an even more promising footballer and was on the books of Sheffield United which was ironic since he spent his Saturdays on the terraces at Hillsborough, home of Sheffield Wednesday. United were in the First Division for much of his time as a schoolboy there and they were keen to offer Savage a contract to stay at the club. The chance of a place with a top flight football club is an offer that most young lads could only dream of, yet for Savage the decision to sign or not was more complex. He had ambitions that extended beyond the game of football, for at the tender age of sixteen and with no realistic expectations of success, Rick was adamant that he was going to be an all-conquering rock musician. With the same swaggering arrogance that characterized the teenage Elliott, Rick felt that it was just a matter of time before he was in a major league band, an even more tempting prospect than playing professional football. Oddly enough, it was a decision that Iron Maiden's founder, bassist Steve Harris, was making at the same time at West Ham United. Savage reasoned that rock music was his first love, that music was much more lucrative in those pre-Premiership days and that the rock'n'roll lifestyle was more fun. You could stay out late, didn't have to worry about what you ate, drank or smoked, while Sheffield United didn't get a lot of action on the groupie front either. Most compelling of all though, it was the hated United rather than his beloved Wednesday that were making him the offer. If Wednesday had come in for his services, who knows? Maybe Def Leppard would never have seen the light of day. Turning his back on the beautiful game, Savage took up an apprenticeship with British Rail, though he never looked on that job as more than a mere time filler until the day stardom beckoned.

While Joe was looking for a break and going to each and every rock gig at Sheffield's City Hall, Rick was taking the first tentative steps towards putting a band together. At the time, Rick's group, in which he played guitar, went under the unappetizing moniker Atomic Mass, a wholly and hopelessly derivative name, centred on heavy metal's preoccupation with horror and holocaust. Alongside him in the band was another local guitarist, Pete Willis. They had met at Tapton Comprehensive School and had been kicking ideas around together since they were fourteen or fifteen. Willis was clearly the more promising of the two on guitar, a more fluent and technically capable player, but if anything it was Savage who remained the driving force behind their dreams. Savage would not be deterred by setbacks while the diminutive Willis was more reserved in his ambitions.

Most school groups crumble when the time to leave comes around, the individuals all going their separate ways, but for some it is the critical moment that propels them forward. Having to get a job merely brought home how ordinary their futures might be and how important the band could be as a launching pad towards better things. Sharing similar tastes to Joe Elliott, Atomic Mass would rehearse a mixture of glam classics and hard rock staples, such that they were never rooted purely in heavy metal but instead had a poppier element to their sound, even at that early stage.

Joe met up with Pete Willis at the school's youth club and when, in 1977, Pete and Rick, along with drummer Tony Kenning, were looking for a singer, Elliott came to mind. At that stage, Joe thought of himself as a guitarist and freely admitted that 'the only singing I'd ever done previously was in the junior school choir. Apart from that,

I once played Elvis Presley in a school play when I was eleven. They only asked me because I was the only person who could play the proper guitar chords to "The Wonder Of You".' But Elliott had made an impression on Willis who recognized in him the same wholehearted commitment that made Savage such a valuable band member. Such was Savage's desire to succeed, he had given up guitar and moved to bass when no suitable bassist could be found, a la Paul McCartney in the post-Sutcliffe Beatles. Nothing would stand in the way of Atomic Mass becoming rock gods, so Rick himself plugged the glaring gap. In the face of that sacrifice, Joe's protestations were easily overcome. After all, he was tall, cut an imposing figure at the front of the stage and wanted out every bit as badly as the others did. Despite making a hash of 'Suffragette City' and 'Stairway to Heaven' at the band's first rehearsal together, Joe was in.

So now they had a four piece, the classic Zeppelin and Sabbath line-up of voice, guitar, bass and drums. Even as teenagers though, the nucleus of Willis, Elliott and Savage could see the limitations of such a rudimentary set-up. Willis in particular felt the band would be restricted if he was the only guitarist and pointed to favourite bands like Thin Lizzy, AC/DC and Judas Priest, all of whom used twin guitars. In fairness to Willis, who is often seen as something of a fall guy in the band's history, his was a very farsighted view for such an inexperienced player and it was also a particularly unselfish one. Given that guitarists are very often the focus of a heavy metal band, over and above the singer, he was choosing to give up much of the spotlight and share it with someone else. Since being in a band is supposedly the best way for a young lad to attract girls and given that Willis was not the most prepossessing physical specimen in the world, it is even more remarkable that he was willing to concede such territory. Clearly with Elliott in place, he too was beginning to feel that Atomic Mass might be on the move and was gripped by the same professionalism that marked those two out.

If they were on the move though, there were still a few things to be sorted out, most notably the name. Atomic Mass was, quite simply, useless. It was hard to imagine posters outside Earl's Court or Madison Square Gardens proclaiming the much awaited return of Atomic Mass. Joe gathered the rest of the lads together in his bedroom for a band meeting. Making the most of the territorial advantage, he resurrected his dream group, Deaf Leopard and suggested that this was a more promising handle for the group. Support was initially muted, but by the end of the evening, Joe had got his way. The only concession he had to make was in the spelling. Def Leppard was born.

2

ALL THE YOUNG DUDES

Creating a successful rock band that can live and work together over a long period is a delicate operation, akin to building a successful football team. Pure blinding talent is not always the vital ingredient, though naturally it's an important element. However, simply putting together a collection of brilliant individuals does not guarantee success, for you can over-egg the pudding and upset the balance. The arrival of Faustino Asprilla at Newcastle United has proved that. If we look back into the late sixties, to the days when super groups were springing up with monotonous regularity, few survived. Most, like Blind Faith for instance, simply fell apart under the weight of powerful egos, combustible characters and individuals who simply didn't get on together.

Balance is the vital and often elusive component of any band with pretensions to longevity and it's why groups that start as an extension of a social life have so much more chance of survival. Genesis began as songwriters at school and while none of them was necessarily a virtuoso musician to begin with, the chemistry within the line-up was right. The same is true of U2, who formed a band as something to do after school. In that light, the omens were always good for Def Leppard. Willis and Savage had met at their comprehensive; they'd run into Joe at their local youth club. Even before they got a band together, a camaraderie existed.

By 1977, they'd all read enough to understand just how important personal relationships were within a group. Ian Hunter's *Diary of a*

Rock'n'roll Star had been published, while interviews in the music press pointed out time and time again that when a band was on tour, the members had to live in one another's pockets for months at a time. Though Willis, Savage and Elliott were very keen to find another guitarist, they were equally concerned that whoever joined their ranks should not upset the chemistry of the group. Once more, fate smiled upon them. Pete Willis was required to attend Stannington College as part of his job as an apprentice lathe operator. Using the opportunity to his own advantage, he used the college library to expand his own knowledge of the guitar, working his way through the technical manuals they had there. It was while he was reading an effects book that Steve Clark introduced himself, the two falling into conversation about their favourite bands, influences and so on. Clark had already worked his way through a few groups, leaving them when it became clear that they lacked the ambition to turn their hobby into a way of life. Again, as he had done with Joe, Willis identified the similarity between Clark's ambition and that of Savage. This time though, he was a little more wary, worried that Clark might not fit in with the group. Equally, now that push had come to shove, perhaps he was having second thoughts about sharing the spotlight with such a supposedly accomplished performer, one who might usurp him in the band.

Clark was not a conventional guitarist by any means. Another Sheffield lad, born in the Hillsborough district on 23 April 1960, he had received his first guitar as a Christmas present from his parents in 1971. The present was given on the understanding that Steve would study the classical guitar and indeed he took a series of lessons, learning pieces from Bach and Vivaldi. By the time he was into his teens though, rock music had taken its hold on his imagination and pretty soon Bach was replaced by Blackmore as a musical hero. Nevertheless the classical lessons had been a vital part of his musical education, providing him with a vocabulary that few contemporary players could equal. It was obvious that here was a precocious talent, greater than that of anyone else in Def Leppard, so it's understandable that Willis should balk at the idea of bringing him into the band. After all, someone like Clark who knew what he was doing might easily eclipse the rest of them and take charge of the whole affair. The two parted after Willis had issued a vague invitation for Clark to come up and see them some time at their rehearsal room above a spoon factory in Bramall Lane.

If Willis was unsure of Clark's value to the band, Joe Elliott had no such reservations. A couple of days after his meeting with Willis, Clark bumped into the two of them in the bar of the City Hall prior to a Judas Priest gig. Following Joe's rather warmer encouragement and impressed by his hopes and dreams for Def Leppard, within a matter of days, on 29 January, Steve was rehearsing with them. Almost at once, he became an integral part of the band, sharing their vision of a glorious future together.

We're forced to return again and again to this incredible self-belief that surrounded Def Leppard, a belief that far outstripped their ability as musicians. They worked tirelessly, trying to play some numbers of their own, always ready to fall back on the classics for a little relief, but as 1978 wore on, rehearsals began to become stale and musical progress was painfully slow. Steve had been in a number of groups that had talked a good game but then failed to do anything about it and it was starting to dawn on him that perhaps Leppard were just another in a long line of time wasters. By the end of June, he had had enough and taking refuge in the Dutch courage offered by several pints of bitter, he told the band that if they didn't start looking for gigs, then he was leaving.

This came as something of a bombshell to the rest of the band who had been content simply to work hard in practice. Joe admitted that 'I panicked because I knew that if Steve left, it could be the end of the band'. Less naturally gifted performers than Clark, they were understandably nervous about making the next leap forward on to the concert stage and there was a general feeling that they weren't ready yet, having been together for just a few months. Steve's decision to quit backed them into a corner and, despite their individual anxieties, they realized that they couldn't take the risk of him leaving the group for he was beginning to show promise as a songwriter too. Clark's game of Russian roulette had paid off and on 18 July, Def Leppard played their first ever concert.

The venue for this earth-shattering event was the gymnasium of Westfield School, the band pocketing the princely sum of five pounds in return for their efforts. The gig itself may have been as low key as they come, but it was absolutely critical in setting Def Leppard on the path they would follow for the next three years, where playing concerts would be central to their strategy. Their performance may well have been ramshackle but it did prove to them that they had something when they played together, that there was a certain quality about them as a band, a spark that separates the men from the boys.

Physically of course, Def Leppard were little more than boys at this stage. Joe was only just approaching his nineteenth birthday, Steve had just turned eighteen while Rick and Pete were just seventeen years old. The naive enthusiasm was enough to keep them going in this early phase of their career, but equally, it did cost them their self respect as they followed the dictates of youthful fashion. As Joe remembered later 'you should have seen the ridiculous clobber we had on to start with! Stripy trousers and leopardskin T-shirts and silk and all that crap. We thought we were very sexy and, of course, we weren't. It's amazing what you think when you're nineteen.' Some of the photographs have survived to tell the tale, turning up regularly in the more unflattering press features on the band.

Sartorially challenged though they might have been, Leppard soldiered on. Having got the taste for live performance at long last, they wanted plenty more of it. Again, they received another stroke of good fortune by virtue of their geographic isolation from London. 1978 was the height of the punk and new wave boom that had supposedly swept away all the old ideas about rock music and replaced them with a brand new order. In London and the south east where the word of the *NME* was law, rock venues were changing their allegiance overnight in order to capitalize on this new movement. Clubs and pubs that had regularly played host to hard rock and heavy metal acts for years on end now refused to look at any band that was not covered in safety pins. If you had long hair, you'd had it. Iron Maiden, for example, had a terrible time finding places to play in London when they were first starting out, Steve Harris fighting an ongoing battle with all manner of promoters just to keep his music alive.

In Sheffield, punk was just another musical fashion that had come along from out of the blue. At a distance of a couple of hundred miles, the punters were less impressed by outlandish clothes and antics and more interested in the product. Indeed, that was very much the story of punk away from the metropolis. Musically it was a breath of fresh air, a wholly necessary chance to take stock of the future direction of rock'n'roll, breaking free of the shackles of pomp rock and insipid pop music. The good bands survived the punk onslaught, those with nothing left to offer died beneath its withering fire. But it's wrong to run away with the notion that punk was rock's 'Year One'. It was anything but, for the new wave was as rooted in the past as any other offshoot of rock'n'roll. Joe Elliott knew his stuff by the time 'Never Mind the Bollocks' was released and his assessment of it was spot on:

> You have to realize that in Sheffield we didn't see the Sex Pistols playing the 100 Club, we didn't get all of those new fanzines, we didn't see Johnny Rotten vomiting down the Kings Road. All we got was the record of 'Anarchy in the UK' in the local record shop at nine o'clock on the Monday morning it came out. We got this already marketed product. And when their album came out, I thought 'This is fuckin' brilliant, heavy rock the way I like it! Ballsy but three chordish'. It had this guy that couldn't sing and a guy that couldn't play solos, but basically it was a rock record. So all the publicity that surrounded punk didn't mean anything. We just had another great rock record to listen to'.

That was the tale through much of provincial Britain. Mohican haircuts remained a pretty rare sight outside the capital and things musical carried on as normal, with the new wave sharing the local scene with more traditional rock bands. For that reason, punk never threatened the evolution of Def Leppard, never had the opportunity to stunt their growth by denying them outlets for their songs. If anything, the punk revolution pushed Def Leppard into the spotlight before they were ready for it, but that's a story for a little later on.

If punk had little obvious musical impact on the band, socio-logically it was more significant. Three-minute songs were back in vogue after years in which no song was worth its salt if it didn't include a three-minute solo. The excesses of progressive rock were brutally hacked back so that rock music had to be concise once again. Indeed, it had to be written in such a way that it might compete in the singles chart, a revolutionary thought given the scorn that bands like Zeppelin and Floyd had heaped upon the Top Twenty. For a rock band, the ideal was now Thin Lizzy or Queen, groups with guts but with an ability to turn out classic rock singles. That was an important shift in emphasis for Leppard, for that was precisely the direction they were heading in, propelled by their collective enjoyment of glam rock.

Punk's other great legacy was the notion that you could do it yourself. A punk band might write a song on Monday, record it on Thursday and have it out in the shops on their own label the following week. The idea of some patriarchal multinational record company deciding what should and shouldn't be released was becoming an outmoded concept as small independent studios began to pop up around the country, offering a decent sound at very reasonable prices. With pressing costs coming down too, a band with a local following could easily record a single, recoup the cost by selling it at their gigs and still have enough copies left to send to radio stations all over Britain.

The unswerving self-belief that Leppard had in themselves and their destiny has already been mentioned on numerous occasions, for that incredible will to win was probably their strongest suit. Running it a very close second was their ability to look two steps ahead of where they were, a knack they have yet to lose. As soon as they had become a live band, they began to consider where they wanted to be six months hence and how they would get there. Getting beyond the confines of Sheffield was the most important step, one which they would accomplish only by succeeding locally and by having some kind of calling card to show to promoters further afield – their own single would do that job very nicely. There's no doubt that that was the next goal they were working towards. They had scarcely left the stage at Westfield School before they had begun to calculate when they would be ready to make that first recording.

Now if punk never became the all-conquering force in the north that it was in London, cities like Sheffield needed their own kind of music, music that could unite teenagers across the city. Like many of the great industrial towns north of Watford such as Birmingham and Newcastle, Sheffield's music of choice was heavy metal and the City Hall hosted shows by all the major members of the metal fraternity. It was a rare week indeed when one rock band or another wasn't packing in 2200 fans. Clearly then, Def Leppard had a base from which to work, a reservoir from which to draw support. Paradoxically though, Sheffield's importance on the metal map made things tougher for them. The people knew their rock music and there were a number of bands trying to break on to the local circuit, playing before crowds that weren't easily impressed – Yorkshire's clubs are to rock bands what Glasgow's are to comedians, a potential graveyard. If that wasn't enough, the very fact that the rock elite were such frequent visitors to the City Hall tended to militate against the smaller clubs. If in any one week you might be able to catch Motorhead, AC/DC and Gillan for instance, you might be less inclined to head off to the Limit or the Leadmill to see a band you'd never heard of on one of your nights off. And woe betide the band whose show happened to clash with Whitesnake's visit to the city, because it'd be liable to end up playing to the proverbial one man and his dog.

The network of working men's clubs that dotted south Yorkshire doesn't immediately appear to offer a particularly promising outlet for an aspiring rock band. Typically of Leppard's attention to detail though, they had evolved a plan in which those clubs were absolutely central. Now out and about on the local circuit, Joe recalled that rock venues offered very little by way of payment: 'After that first show, we played loads of dingy dungeon-type places and got paid about fifteen quid a time. We did the rock pubs for that much and all we could drink but a van would cost us £35 for each gig. When we did the working men's clubs, we got better paid and we'd sign for our money as Mickey Mouse so that we couldn't be traced. Those gigs paid for what we lost while we were trying to break into the rock circuit.' It's a tribute to their versatility that they were able to get such a lot of work in the working men's clubs, not normally regarded as a heavy metal hotbed. Their own songs were in a slightly lighter vein and, by playing covers such as Thin Lizzy's 'Emerald' and 'Rosalie', the Bob Seger song they'd appropriated, they were able to keep those audiences happy. The real test though would come on the rock circuit, as they knew full well.

No-one could accuse the band's members of not working hard enough for, true to their faith, Def Leppard became something of a religion to them. In spite of their day jobs, if they didn't have a gig to play, they'd rehearse for four hours a night, five nights a week as well as on Saturday and Sunday afternoons. Transportation difficulties were finally solved in a novel fashion. Joe Elliott again: 'Eventually, I got the sack from that store-keeping job – I got caught playing cricket in the basement – and I got a job as a van driver which came in very handy!' Surprisingly enough, the delivery van tended to moonlight as Def Leppard's official transport. But even with Leppard's willingness to play anywhere for anything – they supported fellow Sheffield band the Human League at one point – they still found it terribly hard to get gigs, playing a mere handful by the turn of the year. Not that they weren't busy, for along the way they lost drummer Tony Kenning to the clutches of a girlfriend who, understandably enough, did not share the group's enthusiasm for rehearsing nor their unswerving faith in their glittering future. Kenning was replaced by Frank Noon, so the intensive practice schedule was now geared to helping him fit into their overall sound.

What was that overall sound? Opinions vary – Joe Elliott was later to argue that Def Leppard had never been a heavy metal band but rather a commercial rock band. At the time, as an article of faith, Leppard were adamant that they *were* heavy metal. In retrospect, their sound seems very lightweight compared with what we regard as heavy metal now, played by groups such as Metallica or Anthrax. Nevertheless, at the time, bands such as Kiss and Van Halen were indisputably from the HM end of the market and Leppard owed much to both. In terms of stage presentation, still very much in its infancy, they drew on their glam roots, spiced up by references to the effusive showmanship of Dave Lee Roth. Costumes, for example, were nothing if not garish according to Elliott. 'In those days we still thought it was cool to have a perm because Robert Plant and Marc Bolan had curly hair. So I got a perm done and it looked disgusting. We used to wear women's clothes on stage. We used to buy all our clothes from Top Shop and Chelsea Girl. If you want to look a bit different from the audience, you're not going to get it in Burtons, so I was regularly in Top Shop. We couldn't really afford anything else – I only got about £28 a week.' How they survived the working men's club is anyone's guess, but survive they did, prospering too, so much so that by November they were ready to make that all-important debut recording.

3

ON THE CREST OF A NEW WAVE

Having only played seven concerts, Def Leppard probably went into the studio too early in many respects, before they had had the chance to become a road hardened band in the way that contemporaries such as Iron Maiden had. Yet it was prophetic that they should choose to do so, for it foreshadowed the emphasis they would place on the two sides of band life for the rest of their career. Live work could be seen as fun, enjoyable and an important part of the group experience, but it was rehearsing, working on songs, honing them to perfection that was the really important thing. Putting a track down on tape was the only means of guaranteeing immortality, and before it was recorded, each new song had to be just right, hence the hours and hours of practice.

With almost a year of hard rehearsing behind them, the nucleus of Savage, Elliott, Willis and Clark felt that they had put a nice body of songs together, from which they could select the best. It's clear how important it was to them to make a recording and finally, they seemed ready to make the step. Financial considerations were uppermost in their minds and ultimately, Joe had to borrow £148.50 from his dad to enable them to make the short trip to Hull to record three songs at Fairview Studios.

Song selection was crucial, for although they were viewing the recording session as a chance merely to demo some songs, they had greater ambitions for the tapes. Even if it did not turn into the debut single they hoped for, at the very least these songs would be their calling card when they approached booking agents across the country. The first song selected itself. 'Getcha rocks off' was simple, honest to goodness hard rock of a kind that had been especially popular in the early seventies. It's most obvious reference point was Deep Purple, for it bore the hallmarks of their 'Speed king'. No masterpiece by any means, it was indicative of a band that could handle their instruments and were promising songwriters. Despite the reservations of Joe's mum – 'I can't understand why people like it. I think it's horrible' – 'Getcha rocks off' had to be the main track. It was fitting that that should be the case, for the very idea of 'getting your rocks off' was the central plank of Def Leppard's manifesto. They were a good-time band, enjoying playing and loving the chance to escape from the real world for however short a time.

The second track 'Ride into the sun', was in a similar vein. Lyrically, it was all top-down cars, cruising freeways and drive-in movies. Clearly the band had been watching plenty of Hollywood's teen movies and were dreaming of the wide open spaces of America. Given that their songs were written beneath the factory chimneys of South Yorkshire in the midst of a particularly drab year for the British weather, they could hardly be criticized for having these widescreen, technicolour visions of escape to a land of opportunity where the sun always shines. What bunch of British teenagers wouldn't want to go and see the land of the free? At the time, such a lyrical preoccupation barely merited any comment, but very soon, these lyrical leanings would spark controversy, drawing the sharpest of critical comment.

The final choice for the studio was interesting for it showed just how heavy metal had changed over the years, thanks to overseas influences. 'Overture' featured an extended instrumental blow-out, its style, its execution, indeed its very title influenced by Canada's Rush, notably the *2112* album that had proved extremely popular among rock fans. Rush had been able to fuse the fairly basic attacking instincts of metal on to the instrumental intricacy of progressive rock, producing what was a unique hybrid at the time. Def Leppard were obviously impressed by Rush's success, and that's understandable because they were perhaps *the* seminal hard rock band in the mid-seventies. 'Overture' was inevitably a pale imitation, but it did showcase the musical ability within the band. Steve Clark in particular was beginning to create a very interesting and distinctive guitar sound all of his own and in that sense, 'Overture' is the more interesting of the three offerings, showing the greatest promise. Its Achilles heel, as with a number of Leppard's songs, was in the lyrical department. Frankly, they were abysmal, wallowing in the alleged mystique of dungeons and dragons, wizards and high-priests. If punk was right about just one thing, it was that this sort of sub-sci-fi nonsense was now out of place, a fact that even Rush accepted on their 1980 release 'Permanent Waves'. Perhaps Def Leppard were still too young and inexperienced to appreciate that, perhaps they were still proudly displaying their lineage, slavishly copying their predecessors rather than absorbing the lessons and producing their own individual style. Whatever the reasons, there can be no doubt that 'Overture', along with many other early Def Leppard creations was woefully short of lyrical originality.

Even with these reservations, reservations which the headstrong group would never have accepted at the time, they had plenty of reason to be happy with the tape they had produced at the end of their stint at Fairview. At a time when music was at its most nihilistic, when musical accomplishment was supposed to be something to be ashamed of, the band had displayed a promising grasp of the hard rock form with Clark particularly prominent, unleashing an impressive new talent. If Sid Vicious scarcely knew which way up to hold his bass guitar, Def Leppard had illustrated that when the musical tide turned, as turn it must, when the ability to play was revered once more, they would be in the vanguard.

Things had gone so well that there was never any question that the songs would be released as a single. The 'Getcha rocks off' EP was set for local release in January 1979, following the precepts of the DIY punk ethic. Having failed to penetrate the rock circuit, Leppard hoped that the EP would provide them with the kind of profile they needed to help them up on to the next rung of the ladder.

Whatever your feelings about the band, no-one could ever accuse Def Leppard of stupidity. They knew just how crucial the EP was to their hopes of getting the band out of the blocks and running towards stardom on a national scale. Showing the patience for which they were later renowned, they did realize that they had first to conquer the local market, something they had so far singularly failed to do. Even local reviewers were underwhelmed by their charms, as Joe remembered: 'We supported the Human League and a reviewer called us "bludgeon riffola", a complete slag off.' Nevertheless, showing resourceful strength in the face of adversity, 'To show that we didn't care, we picked up on the phrase and used it for the record label'.

Thus 'Getcha rocks off' made its debut on Bludgeon Riffola in January 1979. Starting modestly – a restriction imposed on them by their shoestring budget – they pressed just 150 copies with a cover and signed lyric sheet. Stocks of these were quickly exhausted and within weeks, another 1000 copies were ready for sale. Knowing how important local radio and local record shops might be, they bombarded these with copies of the single. One recipient was Peter Martin who ran Revolution Records; Martin being widely renowned as someone who was only too happy to provide a platform for any local bands that had managed to put out a record. Once he heard Def Leppard's EP, he knew that he was on to something a little different to the generally enthusiastic, energetic, but fatally flawed punk product that he was used to receiving. Never a great punk fan himself, Martin knew that the new wave had already seen its best days. As we entered 1979, it was just a matter of time before the next musical trend emerged. With his livelihood resting on record sales, he also knew the value of the much-maligned 'classic rock' format, a style which though universally derided, still made up a sizeable proportion of his sales. A new, young band in that style certainly had a lot to offer in the years ahead.

Martin sent a copy of the EP on to Frank Stuart-Brown, a well-known local promoter, just the sort of person that Leppard needed to bring on board if they were going to start taking things on to another level. He and Martin had worked together in the past as sales reps for WEA before going their separate ways. Stuart-Brown was now a significant figure on the music scene in the North and, on hearing Leppard's songs, realized immediately that the possibilities were limitless. Over the course of a phone call, the two renewed their friendship and formed a management company, MSB, with a view to guiding the career of Def Leppard. Little more than a bunch of enthusiastic kids trying to find their way through the professional jungle, Leppard were only too happy to listen to the plans put forward by this ambitious duo and a brief band meeting saw them agree to sign up with MSB. Stuart-Brown had already endeared himself to them by playing a tape of the EP to an old colleague, Andy Peebles, who had an evening rock show on Radio 1 from 8 until 10pm. Peebles and his producer Jeff Griffin were every bit as taken with the recording as Stuart-Brown had been. Even at this early stage, Griffin wanted to book the band for a prestigious Radio 1 session. Yet more astonishing, the two of them persuaded the great guru of the new wave, John Peel, to air Leppard's EP on his extremely influential Radio 1 programme. In the late seventies, if Peel was playing your record, those high up in the record industry would be taking very careful note of you.

Although they were just feeling their way into the music industry, the band weren't short of good ideas. Before MSB had arrived on the scene, the group had come up with a shortlist of people who they felt should get a copy of the EP. One such was Geoff Barton, a journalist at *Sounds*. Barton's love of heavy metal, and Kiss in particular was the stuff of newspaper legend. Given that Leppard ploughed a similar glam rock furrow to that of Kiss, Barton seemed an ideal contact. Penning a very straightforward letter, asking him to give them a listen, their lack of pretension and self-promotional bullshit intrigued Barton from the off. Playing the single through, he was the next in a long line of influential figures to hear the sound of a major rock band in the making.

In early 1979, punk was in its death throes had we but known it. Though the *NME* and, to a lesser extent, *Melody Maker* tried to prolong its life, it had entered the terminal phase that any trend faces. The great bands having already made their impact, it was inevitable that the bandwagon-jumpers would follow eagerly in their wake, ever-paler imitations of the Sex Pistols and the Clash, cluttering up the pages with their increasingly desperate attempts to gain publicity. The policy at *Sounds* had always been a little different. Although it too had covered the rise of punk in the minutest detail, it had always kept one foot in the rock camp, continuing to give space to bands that were anathema to the *NME*. Writers such as Barton were tired of having had the new wave rammed down their throats for the preceding couple of years and were looking to find a way of moving the agenda back on to their favoured hard rock territory. In its typically cyclical fashion, it was time for the industry as a whole to reinvent itself, seizing on the glories of a former era. Barton and others felt that the era of the metal bands was ripe for rediscovery and exploitation.

There's no doubt that on a purely commercial basis, the instincts of Barton and those who supported him at *Sounds* were quite correct. Although there was a concerted campaign to make it seem that heavy rock was now thoroughly redundant and had no adherents, all its followers having seen the light and crossed over to punk, that kind of simplification was a long way from the truth. A lot of people had tired of the dinosaur acts of the early seventies, that was why punk had been such a success. But if you looked at any major town or city in the country, you would find that Uriah Heep had just played there, that Whitesnake were coming next week and next month you'd be able to see Hawkwind. In terms of coverage, rock music had gone underground – though paradoxically that added to its allure – but it had never perished. There was a huge groundswell of support just waiting to be tapped by any up and coming band that could breathe new life into heavy metal.

Def Leppard were ideally qualified to make the most of this possible resurgence of interest in their kind of music. If Barton's putative relaunch of the genre was to succeed, he desperately needed standard bearers, a new act around whom he could build his coverage. Leppard were such a band. Relatively photogenic – certainly compared with the rest of the new metal bands of the time – their image had possibilities. Instrumentally they were extremely accomplished and professional while if Joe's voice was something of a weak link, he made up for it with his confident delivery and imposing personality. Their style, if a little clichéd, was instantly recognizable and appealing to rock fans and there was also a pleasingly poppy edge to the material that might allow them to gain some success on the singles charts. All of these were vital ingredients, though London's Iron Maiden might have made very similar claims.

What really distinguished Leppard from the crowd was their extreme youth – Joe, the oldest member of the troupe, was still just nineteen. That made all the difference, for they had no baggage to carry with them; none of them had been in bands before punk came along, none had to hide embarrassing membership of some awful hippy group in 1973. When the new wave had come along, it was supposedly untainted by the past. Def Leppard could claim similarly virginal status for their brand of heavy rock.

That claim was substantiated yet further when Frank Noon, never more than a temporary member of the group, decided to leave the band. A local newspaper ran a story, 'Leppard Loses Skins', along with an advert for a replacement. Sheffield's musical community had another wunderkind at the time, Rick Allen, born on 1 November 1963. This precocious talent had drummed with local group Smokey Blue when he was just a ten year-old but had grown tired of playing drums in his adolescence. It was his father Jeff who first picked up on the article and, failing to coax his son into contacting the band, called Def Leppard himself. He finally arranged for Rick to meet up with Steve and Joe and, over the course of a long conversation, it became clear that Allen was the boy for the job, being offered – and accepting – the position without the need for an audition. He left school to join the band because 'my mum and dad told me I was never going to get another opportunity like this'. Angus Young might dress like a schoolboy with AC/DC, but Leppard went one better. They had a real schoolboy in their band!

None of these developments made any dent in Barton's desire to feature Def Leppard. The problem was that, as a writer based in London and working on *Sounds*' editorial staff, it was difficult for him to find time to see Leppard in action. Given that they had yet to play outside their locale – and they played infrequently even there – it was an insuperable obstacle for some little time. By the time he did get to see them in the early Summer of 1979, Def Leppard already had the rock world interested in them.

A lot of the credit has to go to the MSB management. They were heavily criticized later in the group's career, but they worked long and hard to get things moving for the group and that merits attention. In May, they ensured that another 15,000 copies of 'Getcha rocks off' were pressed and sold, guaranteeing that the record would be available all over the country, being played in rock discos the length and breadth of the land. Like Iron Maiden's 'Soundhouse tapes', Leppard's debut offering featured regularly in the *Sounds* Heavy Metal charts, spreading their name further and further afield.

With the success of that EP came recognition in Sheffield. Picking up on the buzz of anticipation that surrounded this group that had suddenly emerged from nowhere, Hallam Radio's Colin Slade offered them their first session, Slade having been the first person anywhere to play the EP on the radio at the start of the year. This they accepted with alacrity for not only was it excellent exposure for their music, it offered them invaluable experience in a recording studio. The five songs, recorded in May 1979, were 'Answer to the master', 'Glad I'm alive', 'When the walls came tumbling down', 'Sorrow is a woman' and 'Beyond the temple'.

Things were really on the up and up now, with MSB having a prominent part to play. Stuart-Brown continued to lean on his friendship with Andy Peebles, getting the DJ to broadcast the EP on Radio 1 quite regularly. Finally, the call came from Broadcasting House to record their first session for Peebles. These recordings were to be made in the BBC's Manchester, rather than London studios, and were to be produced by Jeff Griffin. In one of those nice coincidences that crop up from time to time, Leppard were set to record on 7 June 1979, for transmission over four days beginning on 18 June, the very week when Geoff Barton's debut feature on the group would run in *Sounds*. The session went especially well, four songs being recorded without undue difficulty, the band clearly benefiting from their practice-run at Hallam. They chose to play 'Wasted', 'Answer to the master', 'Glad I'm alive' and 'Sorrow is a woman', three of which would make it to their debut album. That in itself was significant for in the month that separated the two sessions, they had clearly decided that a song like 'Beyond the temple' was simply too outdated for consideration, yet had produced 'Wasted' which was a lot closer to the pop rock sound that they would go on to patent. With its Kiss-like sound, you might even think they'd written it in honour of Geoff Barton's visit. Whatever the case, Def Leppard were on a roll now, producing songs with ease, constantly updating and improving their repertoire so that they would be ready when the call came from the majors. For come it surely would.

It was the neat synchronicity of the Peebles session and the *Sounds* feature that changed the lives of Elliott, Willis, Savage, Clark and Allen for good. By the end of June, they were the hottest unsigned property in Britain. Geoff Barton's feature was rhapsodic, so unerringly favourable that they might have written it themselves. Def Leppard produce 'high powered heavy rock played to a degree of tightness usually only achieved after a half dozen gruelling American tours' he wrote, making it clear that the band had his unequivocal support.

Sounds were about to pin their colours to the mast of a new musical movement, the fabled 'New Wave of British Heavy Metal', the NWOBHM. For those on the staff who shared Barton's musical tastes, this was no hardship for it gave them the opportunity to report on the music closest to their hearts. More important though was the editorial stance on the situation. Britain's three weekly music papers – the *NME, Melody Maker* and *Sounds* – were locked into a fairly restricted market place and the competition for circulation between the three was fierce, the rivalry intense. By becoming the first paper to distance itself from punk, *Sounds* was taking something of a gamble, hoping that in offering a clear alternative to the two, it might attract a new readership who had become bored with the tribal loyalties of punk. If the NWOBHM was going to give *Sounds* that edge, it needed a focal point. There were countless new metal bands doing the rounds at that stage and Def Leppard were not the best known by any means. Iron Maiden, Samson, the Tygers of Pan Tang and several others had claims to a wider audience than Leppard. Yet, as already noted, Leppard were the group that had everything to offer, notably a potentially commercial sound where groups like Angelwitch were still turning out music that was solely rooted in the past. Def Leppard were the chosen band.

It was ironic that they should be selected to head up the NWOBHM for, even at their inception, they were not really heavy metal, certainly not by any definition that the music's true adherents would recognize. They owed far more to Thin Lizzy than they did to Black Sabbath and their attitude and live performance was purposely transatlantic, their tentative attempts at a glamourous presentation clearly having been influenced by Van Halen and Kiss. Quite simply, Leppard were in the right place at the right time, their FM sound appealing to Barton and company who wanted to extinguish the flames of punk rock.

Not that Leppard were averse to kicking punk in the teeth either. Steve Clark reckoned that it had had its day: 'Young kids used to be into new wave because it was new, but it isn't any more. Now there's as many young kids into heavy metal – probably more – as there are into punk.' Rick Savage agreed with the thrust of that argument, inadvertently putting a careerist spin on his words that would come back to haunt them: 'We're not into punk. We were all heavy rock fans before we formed this band. I can listen to punk, I thought the Pistols were brilliant, it's just that we all grew up on heavy rock and we're anxious to keep it going. If we did play punk rock, we might disappear without trace because everybody's doing it now.' The fear of disappearing without trace made it seem as if Leppard had merely chosen heavy rock as a vehicle to get success rather than out of an abiding respect for the music. It was merely a case of someone not used to doing interviews being unable to say precisely what he wanted, but it sowed the first seeds of doubt as to Leppard's motives.

For the moment, that was glossed over as readers were taken aback by the astonishing confidence displayed by these youngsters. Joe Elliott was particularly keen to put the band's point of view across, exaggerating the invincibility they seemed to possess as a unit with a piece of breathtaking impudence. 'Van Halen came across riding on top of this vast publicity thing. If we had the publicity, we could do as well if not better than them.' Since Van Halen were being touted as rock's great white hope, feted with fawning reviews and had just enjoyed four million sales of *Van Halen II* in the States, with a ten month world tour to accompany it, this seemed to be taking self-confidence into the realms of fantasy but as Joe remarked later, 'I knew Def Leppard would be successful, even though we were rubbish when we first started. I just knew we had something'.

With the *Sounds* piece alerting the record industry to Leppard's prowess, by the end of June, with their first Radio 1 session broadcast amid a buzz of eager anticipation, a chorus of record companies was paying court to the band. Fortunately, with this media success behind them, they were able to play more frequently, allowing an assortment of A&R men to see them in the flesh, to see what they were made of. Certainly, Leppard weren't backward in coming forward, Savage memorably evoking their on-stage charms: 'We're just doing what we want to do. Basically it's just down to the fact that we're all fucking posers. We all want to go out on stage, pose, wear dinky white boots, tight trousers and have all the girls looking at our bollocks. That's us. That's it. We're arrogant bastards.'

Live shows in Sheffield's smaller venues were undeniably impressive and the group's naive enthusiasm carried them through any technical shortcomings they might have had, notably the fairly rudimentary nature of Joe's voice, though he argued strenuously in his defence that 'if it's perfect live, it's boring'. As a frontman though he was engaging – essential given that the rest of the band lacked any real visual impact, Willis being especially introverted. Even so, there was a certain panache about the group, Rick Allen remarking that 'we try to look good, we try to have some style'. Even if their stage clothes were misguided to say the least – the chubby Elliott might try to squeeze his ample frame into some imitation leather trousers for instance – it did at least prove that unlike the rest of the metal bands who dressed in the regulation jeans and T-shirts like their fans did, Def Leppard might not be averse to an industry image make-over. That, allied to their youth, certainly suggested that a powerful record company might be able to manipulate the band, pushing them in certain industry-friendly directions without too much difficulty. A final showcase gig at the Porterhouse in Retford clinched things for Leppard. The band's desire to succeed was palpable and if a company could persuade them that it knew best, it would be so much easier than dealing with the stroppy 'idealists' that punk had occasionally – very occasionally – thrown up. Def Leppard, much as they loved their music and their lifestyle, were hard headed pragmatists. They wanted success, wanted a career and accepted the fact that they needed to sell records worldwide. They were clearly willing to do all that was necessary to achieve their goals. In the summer of 1979, they looked like a record company's dream, a straightforward band that wanted the big time and were ready for the long haul.

4

INTO THE FIRE

By August 1979, Def Leppard could have signed with any of half a dozen major record labels. Finally, after discussion between themselves and the MSB management duo, they opted to go with Phonogram, signing to their Vertigo label, the home of Thin Lizzy among others. The final advance sounded extremely generous – £100,000 for a band with just a few dozen gigs to its name, playing in a style that had supposedly been killed off by punk. In truth, Phonogram were playing things cagily, for the advance actually worked out at just £20,000 per annum for five years, in order to cover the costs of recording – what a major miscalculation that turned out to be! Clearly then, the members of Def Leppard did not become rich men overnight and their lifestyle barely changed.

Why were Leppard the first of the new metal bands to get a major deal? It is impossible to pretend that they were light years ahead of the competition for the recorded evidence suggests little to choose between 'Getcha rocks off' on the one hand and Iron Maiden's 'Soundhouse tapes' on the other, while the NWOBHM sampler that followed all the media activity in early 1980 – 'Metal for muthas' – indicates that a number of bands were every bit as musically proficient as Leppard were at the time. There must have been more to Phonogram's decision than ability alone.

The *Sounds* article had obviously got the A&R men interested and that was a distinct advantage, for other NWOBHM articles had tended to be based on live shows where three or four bands had played, each consequently winning just a fraction of the coverage accorded Leppard. With *Sounds* standing foursquare behind them, Phonogram knew that the band had friends in the right places, making their marketing job that little bit easier. Yet Def Leppard brought with them some baggage that was not to the company's taste. For instance, though he was a personable and hugely likeable character, Joe Elliott's voice was, at this stage, useless. Metal music does not always require a vocalist with the range of a Paul Rodgers or a Robert Plant, and some very average singers have survived in the field, making a very good living in the process. Even so, having a singer who couldn't hold a note in a very large bucket is not generally considered to be a good thing. By punk standards, Elliott was a positive Pavarotti, but by the standards of 1975, when hard rock had still been ruling the musical roost, he was depressingly inadequate. To be fair to Joe, it was a failing that he was big enough to acknowledge later on in the band's career, though at the time, he and his band mates defended his vocal style to the hilt as indeed they had to.

Neither were Def Leppard the most attractive band, especially once they'd burdened themselves with their ludicrous Top Shop stage garb and atrocious perms. The bubble headed Elliott made Kevin Keegan's seventies experiments with his own coiffure look distinguished, Allen still looked like a kid behind the drums while the group's youth was emphasized by the elfin features of Willis. In truth, Leppard were a band of all the averages compared with the great rock bands of a previous era. They looked like a bunch of average young blokes, their songwriting offered little that was surprising and their playing was strictly 'good enough' at this stage. The only thing exceptional about them was their age and their ambition. That was enough.

So the key question once again. Why were Leppard signed up so quickly? The only logical answer is that they had time on their side, they had some potential, they were the right band to fill the gaping hole that existed in the marketplace and, most importantly, they wanted it badly enough. Their youth was vitally important to Phonogram for a number of reasons. Not having had the time to get to know the band very well, Phonogram's top brass jumped to the obvious conclusion that any hard-nosed business executive would when confronted with what looked like a group on a school field trip; we can control them. It was an impression that was strengthened by their tangible determination to become a major league rock act. If they're that keen, runs the argument, they'll do anything we tell them.

Their youthful innocence was equally important when one remembered just why punk had come along in the first place. Bands had been populated by men approaching middle age, at least in rock'n'roll terms. Some members of Wishbone Ash were over thirty for heaven's sake! It all added to the impression of tired old music, made by tired old men, recycling the same tired old ideas. Punk had conspired to make heavy rock look geriatric, yesterday's music. If you were going to try to sell that to a new generation of kids, you had to have a new generation of heroes. Given that monkey glands could not give the gift of eternal youth to Led Zeppelin and their ilk, heavy metal needed a transfusion of new blood. It needed a group of youngsters who had lived through the punk era and had still chosen hard rock as their medium to give it a shot in the arm, to reinvigorate a dying art. As Elliott pointed out with uncanny accuracy, 'there must be a new generation of heavy metal fans, people who must be pissed off with listening to bands that were formed over twelve years ago like Zeppelin and Black Sabbath . . . they want somebody young'. It would not have been possible to find a more youthful, enthusiastic, energetic and altogether unsullied bunch than Def Leppard, so they became the chosen ones.

Finally, their age, demeanour and predisposition towards 'glamorizing' their music opened up a whole new market – the female audience. Hard rock had always been an almost exclusively male preserve with only Led Zeppelin and the chest-beating antics of Robert Plant enticing girls to their gigs. Joe Elliott remarked that 'I went to all the rock gigs at the City Hall from 1976 to 1980, there'd be 2200 people there, with about thirty or forty girls'. No 'new man', Joe offered his considered opinion as to why this was: 'Our music's too masculine for girls. They tend to crumble under the pressure. Girls don't buy the records, they only buy Boney M and Bay City Rollers singles.' If he didn't want girls at their gigs, the idea of some kind of crossover was doubtless rather more than a gleam in an excited marketing man's eye. If a rock band could sell 300,000 albums for example while only appealing to a male audience, how many might they sell if you could get girls interested too? Any band able to do that would instantly double its potential audience. This incontestable piece of accountancy was to reach its fulfilment with the arrival of Jon Bon Jovi and his cheekbones, but Def Leppard were midwives to the idea, there at its birth. With such baby-faced band members as Allen and Willis, Leppard's 'cute quotient' was undeniable.

Such preoccupations at Phonogram HQ made it very obvious that Def Leppard had not been signed merely to slog around the Odeon circuit, releasing biannual albums that did very nicely in the UK but meant nothing anywhere else. Phonogram's whole marketing strategy revolved around putting Leppard on the world market, notably in the States, the world's music supermarket. If you can make it there, you don't need to make it anywhere (else) to paraphrase Mr Sinatra.

The band themselves were not exposed to such revolutionary thinking so early in the day. Even at Phonogram, this may well have been mere pie in the sky idealism, hopes that might be unrealizable. But America was very much on the agenda as far as the record company was concerned. Elsewhere however, such grandiose ideas had never been considered. For MSB, there was a quite different set of priorities, for they were working to a wholly different rule book.

Def Leppard as a unit had received a huge boost in the light of Phonogram's still-substantial investment and they were given the scope to pack in the day job and concentrate solely on the band and on songwriting. But it wasn't merely their efforts that were being rewarded. Martin and Stuart-Brown could afford themselves a pat on the back for taking their charges from nowhere to international recording artists in the space of eight short months – no mean achievement. Sadly for MSB though, personal relations between them and the group were beginning to deteriorate. Though both Martin and Stuart-Brown had some experience of the periphery of the music industry, neither had been involved at the core before, nor had either of them managed a band in the past. MSB was essentially a 'fly by the seat of your pants' operation, the two evolving their own ground rules as they progressed, just as Def Leppard were. In truth, it's very,

very difficult to criticize MSB, for they did get Leppard the contract they wanted and a reasonably favourable deal in the process – they picked up an industry-standard royalty of 10 per cent, perfectly acceptable for an unknown group.

Despite Leppard's 'overnight success' and the part MSB had in it, murmurings of discontent started to surround them. Personality clashes did not help matters, but others in the group's entourage began to wonder aloud if perhaps Def Leppard didn't need a more experienced management outfit, and if things could not be run a little more professionally. Much of the discontent seemed to originate with Phonogram who, feeling that the boys in the band might be willing to do their bidding, were not keen on having to deal with managers who had very clear ideas of their own. Impressionable youngsters still, despite their own belief in themselves, Leppard started to take some of these criticisms to heart.

Things began to go downhill for MSB almost as soon as Def Leppard had inked the contract. Though they were now signed up to one of the biggest labels in the world, the band were still very much musical novices, certainly as far as live shows went. Their approach to their career so far had been a softly, softly one, doggedly pursuing and then achieving one goal before moving on to another. For Stuart-Brown, the danger was that now they had a deal, the pace of events might run away with the band, leaving them cruelly exposed. He wanted to accompany the Phonogram re-release of 'Getcha rocks off' with a low-key tour on the 'toilet' circuit, bringing the band face to face with the fans who would make up their hard-core audience. He was only too well aware that having released such a popular single, having recorded a successful Radio 1 session, and been the subject of enthusiastic coverage in *Sounds*, Leppard were now anointed as the number one band in the NWOBHM fold, and were being greeted with almost messianic fervour by the heavy metal hoardes. Stuart-Brown strongly suspected, with good reason, that when the time came for Leppard to deliver the goods, they would be found wanting. That was why a club tour was such a great idea in his view. It's far easier to play a memorable gig in the intimate atmosphere of the Marquee Club where 250 committed punters are bathed in their own sweat than in the cavernous atmosphere of Hammersmith Odeon where you know you'll have your work cut out just to get the crowd on your side. With the benefit of hindsight, MSB were probably right.

Phonogram, on the other hand, weren't interested in such niceties. They filled the group's heads with stories of their importance and popularity, boosting their collective ego at every turn. Never short of confidence, pretty soon Def Leppard had every reason to believe they were unstoppable. They wanted to play to as many people as they could as quickly as they could, spreading the gospel about themselves. And so it was that they found themselves playing their first national tour in Odeon-sized venues as support to America's Sammy Hagar.

It should be remembered that with the exception of the Porterhouse showcase, Leppard had never made any concerted attempt to venture any further afield than their own backyard, gigs where they would be comforted by the sight of familiar faces in the small audiences. Having signed to Phonogram, the idea of a year spent slogging away in the clubs and pubs was disheartening, because they already felt they were better than that, the more so because an enticing alternative was being dangled before their eyes by their friendly record company. Reflecting on these early days later, Joe admitted that 'nobody could tell us anything, we thought we knew it all'. Such brashness can be a mighty weapon, but it can lead to its fair share of problems.

It was inevitable that their ideas would begin to diverge from those of MSB, for by the autumn of 1979, they were looking at wholly different objectives, Leppard understandably excited by Phonogram's global agenda. MSB were a little too rooted in the past, gradually unfolding a masterplan that had now been superseded, failing to recognize that the British market had shrunk while it was becoming far easier to break into overseas territories. MSB's rationale was to make Def Leppard a respected and admired group in the UK, reasoning that if they had a solid base from which to work, they could tackle the rest of the world with confidence. Their wholly excusable error was to think that such an inexperienced band would be hopelessly out of their depth in America, that they would have to 'pay their dues' in the UK for a couple of years, get a couple of solid albums under their belt, learn how to be a professional band and step up the pace gradually. Def Leppard laboured under no such misapprehension, certain that they were ready for whatever challenges the rest of the world might throw at them. Remarkably, almost unbelievably, they were right, but in fairness to MSB, they'd shown no indication that that would be the case.

MSB were using the pre-punks as a prototype, artists like Thin Lizzy and Genesis, who built steadily and surely via gigs in their home country before taking off to attack markets elsewhere in the world. In that regard, they had mounted a quite superb campaign, in tandem with Leppard's own ideas. The 'Getcha rocks off' EP had won massive exposure given its humble origins, while the way in which the Peebles session and the *Sounds* feature coincided was a masterstroke. Even if it had been a complete accident – and there are differing opinions on that – it was the kind of good fortune that establishes reputations. Their ability to keep their eyes fixed firmly on the ball was amply illustrated again when the group were given another BBC session, this time with Tommy Vance's Friday Rock Show, *the* premier hard rock radio show in the UK. Recorded with Vance's producer Tony Wilson in the Maida Vale studios on 3 October for broadcast on the 26th of that month, the band ran through 'Satellite', 'Rock brigade', 'Wasted' and 'Good morning freedom', illustrating that they were keen to rehearse, in a studio environment, those songs that would be cornerstones of their debut album. Once more, the session was well received by a wide cross-section of the metal fraternity and added a little more fuel to the fires of publicity.

As far as the UK was concerned, Def Leppard really were the new Messiahs, returning to lead metal into a new golden age. Reviews in *Sounds* were uniformly jubilant, those BBC sessions were among the most requested for repeat broadcast and on the back of all that, 'Getcha rocks off' continued to sell, eventually shifting around 30,000 copies after Vertigo re-released it in September. Def Leppard were Britain's favourite rock band. MSB had achieved all of their major objectives in the first phase of their overall strategy. It was all they were given the chance to do. Unhappy with the Hagar tour, they were distraught when the band were booked on to AC/DC's tour as special guests, playing at such atmosphere-free zones as Stafford's

Bingley Hall. MSB made it clear that they felt this was a mistake when to the band, it was the fulfilment of everything they'd been working for. The writing was already on the wall, a fact that was merely underlined when the band met up with Peter Mensch who worked for AC/DC's management and was looking for a band of his own – Leppard's prestigious guest slot on the tour had come about largely at his instigation. The seeds of a new business relationship were sown there and then, though they did not come to fruition until a little later in the band's career.

In the meantime, they'd released their first pukka Vertigo single, the Kiss-style stomp of 'Wasted', produced by Nick Tauber, highlighting the commercial potential of the line-up. Tauber's production skills seemed suited to the band thanks to his strong pop sensibility – something that he demonstrated later with Marillion – but he was not thought to possess the right hard rock credentials to handle the album, for it was vital that Leppard did not shy away from the NWOBHM bandwagon at this early juncture. At the end of the decade, their best hope for success seemed to be beneath the umbrella of hard rock.

As a consequence, Tom Allom was called in to produce, sessions taking place in Ascot's Startling Studios through the first part of December 1979, their basic work completed in a mere eighteen days. Allom had already earned respect, with Joe particularly happy with his work on Judas Priest's 'Unleashed in the East', citing this as the clinching reason for Allom's selection.

Looking back at rock records from the late seventies and early eighties is a difficult business, not least because of the fact that groups like Def Leppard revolutionized the way contemporary records sound. Many of the considerable shortcomings of 'On Through the Night' can be put down to its atrocious sonic quality, which gives the music all the impact of a damp sock attacking a rice pudding. Perhaps Allom was at fault in some respects – his attempts at making 'Getcha rocks off' which seem to have been recorded live, and live in America at that, were incredibly amateurish and totally inexcusable. The real problem, though, came in trying to make a record in those days, where the studio environment was caught at a turning point, a halfway house that did no-one any favours. Recording had moved on from the naive charm and simplicity of the 1960s. Basic technical innovations had robbed record makers of the need to use their ingenuity in the way that George Martin and the Beatles had at Abbey Road. By 1979 you could get the effects that they'd worked on for days in a matter of minutes as recording desks had moved on from four and eight-track to a more customary sixteen or twenty-four track facility. In that sense, many musicians and producers had lost their exploratory verve, now they were no longer relying on technology that wasn't up to the job. Of course, in the mid-eighties, Def Leppard demonstrated just how far things had moved on when they grabbed hold of 1980s technology and bent it to their will, making records that were dramatically different to anything that rock had heard before, at least in terms of the texture of the sound. Stuck in Startling Studios in 1979, they may have believed that the equipment there was state of the art, but sadly, that art was in a state and the record lost out accordingly.

You can't blame all its deficiencies on the production facilities however, for Def Leppard were a long way from being the new musical genii that the public had been told to expect. Any album that opened with a song as moronic as 'Rock brigade' was in serious trouble from the outset. It was nice and bright, filled with enthusiastic vigour, but that was its only charm, for it was adolescent rubbish, a flush of excitement that they were in a band that was out on the road. Clearly they fancied it as their signature, Def Leppard, the 'Rock brigade', coming to your town soon – the theme tune from 'The Monkees' but without any of the musical accomplishment or tongue-in-cheek humour.

On through the night continued in similarly lacklustre vein, with the lyrical disasters coming thick and fast. If 'Wasted' was musically competent, the sound of the young Elliott boasting of downing bottles of whisky was bizarre in the extreme. The same was equally true of 'It could be you', Elliott's attempt to out-Gillan Ian Gillan, regaling his audience with tales of groupies. Where Gillan did it with panache, a wink and a smile, letting the crowd in on the joke, Elliott's delivery was riven with cliché, as if he genuinely believed all this rubbish, and when that was added to a stumbling, echoey chorus, you had a thorough mess. 'Satellite' was inconsequential, the kind of wild axe blow-out that any half-decent rock band with a Judas Priest or AC/DC album in their collection could have knocked off in half an hour.

'Answer to the master' offered the band the chance to introduce some more interesting time changes that were similar to those employed by Rush, while 'Sorrow is a woman', Leppard's attempt at showcasing a 'sensitive' side, ushered in by some acoustic playing, flopped woefully. Boasting the abysmal squelchy drum sound that ruined most records at the time, a sound that persisted until Phil Collins and Peter Gabriel almost reinvented drumming for Gabriel's third solo LP, its heavy-handed atmospherics were unconvincing in the extreme, as Elliott's voice veered towards Ozzy Osbourne, totally unsuited to a track of that kind.

'When the walls came tumbling down' was the absolute nadir, dabbling in the hackneyed visions of Armageddon that Sabbath had been dealing in for years, adding nothing new or interesting to the genre, its ludicrous spoken introduction and Joe's unnatural American accent compounded the original sin of its composition.

That leaves the few saving graces of a record which wallowed in the outdated excesses of hard rock. 'It don't matter' was illuminated by a bluesier, more reflective guitar figure than had been used elsewhere, and if the lyrics remained unexceptional, instrumentally it was perhaps the most interesting piece on the album. Ironically, it vied for that distinction with a song called 'Hello America', a track that was to cause them more heartache than anything else they would record. Opening in an almost Queen-like fashion, it was distinctly unmetallic in tone, even using synthesizers, anathema still to most rock bands in 1979. Queen themselves had only just started to embrace them, despite having defiantly noted that there were 'no synthesizers' on their early recordings. If only because it was something unexpected, 'Hello America' stood out, while Elliott gave his best vocal performance with a decent take on Robert Plant's phrasing.

Like pretty well everything else on *On through the night*, the song suffered through the lack of attention that had been paid to the lyrics, lyrics which gave a stereotypical view of the United States, all freedom, Greyhound buses and wild times in San Francisco. Mindless fun, inconsequential and a bit of a laugh you might think. Joe Elliott certainly thought so, explaining that 'it was just a song about wanting to visit America and see all the places you see on film. I used to work on a treadmill, making knives and forks; it doesn't cross over into a lyric. There's nothing in Sheffield to write songs about. You can't write "This is steel city" and mean it. It'd come across like a bloody heavy metal Hovis ad!'

That was fair comment to a degree but punk had shown that you could be socially conscious and still be lyrically engaging or enigmatic according to taste. Willis did not agree, arguing that 'everybody's got problems. If you want to go to a concert and hear about "life on the dole" then that's up to you, but it were never my idea of a show'. It is of course a matter of personal opinion as to whether or not groups should become politicized, and there are strong arguments from either side of the fence. In early 1980, with musically inspired movements such as Rock Against Racism in full swing, singing about those old topics of wine, women and song seemed almost distasteful to some and Def Leppard were immediately picked out by the right-on, politically correct press as vacuous airheads, the sort of band that punk should have exterminated.

Leppard had little reason to worry about such matters though, for they had clearly found their constituency. *Sounds'* Christmas issue included the annual opportunity to vote in the paper's poll, in categories such as best band, best singer, best new band and so on. When the results were finally published in March, Def Leppard's success could not have been anticipated. They won the Best New Band category with some ease, a pleasing performance, if not entirely unexpected. What was astonishing was that they carried off the prize for Best Single too with the 'Getcha rocks off' EP. The poll may not have been the most scientifically compiled sample in the world, but it certainly pointed to a band in the ascendant. With '*On Through the Night*' set to come out just a few weeks later, the omens could not have been better. Except . . .

5

WITH A LITTLE HELP FROM OUR FRIENDS

The *Sounds* poll victory should have been the cause of much celebration in the Def Leppard camp, final vindication for the two years of hard labour they'd put in since Steve Clark had joined. Unfortunately, there was a two month time lag between voting taking place and the results being announced, and if a week is a long time in politics, two months in as fickle a business as rock'n'roll is a veritable eternity. Votes had been cast when Leppard were at the pinnacle of British acceptance. The results came when the wheels had fallen off the intergalactic juggernaut that (dis)graced the sleeve of their debut album.

What the media gives, the media can also take away. If *Sounds* had been instrumental in getting the band a contract, in promoting them across the country and in turning them into the most hotly tipped new band since the Clash, it was equally pivotal when the walls came tumbling down around them. Stupidly enough, their demise was started by the release of a single which achieved their first Top Fifty chart placing. 'Hello America' heralded a remarkable reverse in fortunes.

The whole sorry affair was symptomatic of a greater malaise at the heart of the Leppard machine. As we've already seen, MSB's days with the band were coming to a close. The rights and wrongs of the situation are complex, there's no obvious objective viewpoint. What it boiled down to in the end was that Leppard's inexhaustible demands and overriding ambition would, they felt, be better served by new management. There has to be considerable sympathy for MSB, having taken their charges to the brink of stardom, but Def Leppard are a strikingly unsentimental band. Feeling that MSB had outlived their usefulness, they had no compunction in getting rid of them, particularly once Mensch had entered the picture. Joe admitted that 'it was when we were supporting AC/DC that Peter Mensch made it obvious to us that he wanted to manage the band. We realized our old management were out of their depth'.

Ironically, though Mensch and his partner Cliff Burnstein, an A&R man at Mercury Records in New York, were keen to represent Def Leppard, they fought shy at first, disturbed by the ethical question that surrounds poaching another manager's artists. An illustration of Leppard's desperation to get the two savvy Americans on their case came when Rick Allen persuaded Mensch to listen in on one of MSB's meetings with the group. Holding a glass to the wall, Mensch was allegedly shocked by the lack of organization or any coherent plan shown by MSB. This apparently helped Mensch overcome any feelings of guilt that he might have had, and very soon after, Def Leppard were being managed by him and Cliff Burnstein.

It was an ideal match in many ways, for band and management shared the same objectives. Joe Elliott remarked that 'we've always wanted to be something that we probably never will be and that's a legend. There are certain bands that people, whether they like them or hate them, have a certain respect for. Bands like Led Zeppelin. Zeppelin are the blueprint'. Peter Mensch was in total agreement, saying 'the bottom line was always to be the next Led Zeppelin or Queen, something with longevity'.

No-one could suggest that Burnstein and Mensch were lacking in originality, in ambition, or in ideas or the future. However, their experience was almost entirely Stateside and they had little appreciation of the UK scene nor grasp of the many nuances that can make or break a band in this most credibility conscious of markets. People in Britain are generally slow to warm to naked ambition, prefer artists who remain close to their roots and behave with a degree of humility. Natural modesty was never one of Leppard's strong suits, their utter confidence in themselves often striking a jarring note in conversation. To profess that what they really wanted was to be successful, rich and famous was simply too vulgar, not the way we do things here at all, the more so in those immediate post-punk days. When Joe argued that 'no matter how much a new wave band says "We're only like the kids", they'd be millionaires if they could', it was akin to heresy, even though there was more than a grain of truth in it. Such ambition raised hackles as well as suspicions.

Though they had finally played smaller venues in early 1980, the ease with which they'd hopped on to tours by Hagar and AC/DC upset many and there were plenty of seasoned rock observers who would have been only too happy to see Def Leppard fail, for they were viewed as cocky upstarts, only in it for the money and with no real ties to the metal movement. Such statements by Elliott were grist to their mill as was the decision to replace MSB with Mensch. If this didn't make their greed apparent to all, what would? More importantly, it was a very clear signal that the band saw their future across the Atlantic rather than at home and that they would do anything, no matter how demeaning, to be successful there. Given that virtually anything that succeeded in America was almost instantly dismissed as trash and bereft of any merit over here, such a move was not going to win them many friends. At the start of February 1980, such sentiments were barely kept under control by the commitment the band put into their stage shows which, along with their general good humour, tended to win over the doubters.

On 21 February, the roof fell in. In a move which betrayed an amazing lack of judgement, they released 'Hello America' as a single in a blaze of publicity. The song was pleasant enough, if not really indicative of the material on *On through the night*, but it was the lyrical subject matter that made waves. The song was discussed in the previous chapter, a travelogue through the most redolent place names in America. Normally it would mean little to anyone, but at a time when the gossipmongers were suggesting that Leppard were about to jump ship and run off to America, it was a startlingly insensitive choice. Since 'Hello America' was also removed from typical hard rock sounds, it was used as evidence that Def Leppard were wimping out in order to win American FM radio acceptance. To the music press, who try to set themselves up as the Jiminy Cricket of the recording industry, the conscience that guides bands away from the dangers represented by the major labels, accepting decisions foisted upon you is a heinous crime, evidence of a complete lack of principles.

Clearly Mick Middles in *Sounds* thought that to be the case. In a review that changed the course of Leppard's career in Britain, he wrote 'if Def Leppard hadn't been thrown into the wacky whirlpool of showbiz heavy metal they would still be making naive but hard-edged youthful rock songs. They once had the power to penetrate but unfortunately their complete trust in the business has rendered them useless'. Erstwhile supporter Geoff Barton followed the same tack the following week when the band had their first *Sounds* front cover to celebrate scooping the reader's poll, suggesting that the Def Leppard he had known and loved were no more. Since *Sounds* was the bible of NWOBHM followers, such devastating critiques inflicted mortal blows on the group's standing in the UK.

If the management had not seen the potential damage that might accrue, Elliott had, but all too late. Responding to accusations that Def Leppard were mere puppets in the hands of the record company, he was forthcoming, if unconvincing.

'We wanted "Rock Brigade" to be the single and when it turned out to be "Hello America", we were a little annoyed but we thought "well, okay, maybe Phonogram know best, maybe it's an equally commercial song". What really did get us uptight were the adverts in the music press. They didn't state that the B-side, "Good Morning Freedom", isn't going to be on the album and, worst of all, they didn't make it clear that it's a re-recorded version of "Hello America", that it's not the same as the song Nick Tauber produced for the flip of "Wasted". But we don't really want to fall out with the record company. Right now, our priority is to be as successful as everybody else on Vertigo like Dire Straits, Thin Lizzy and Status Quo and if we start getting awkward . . .'

That of course merely compounded the felony in most eyes. The band hadn't agreed with the decision, but they let it go without a fuss because they didn't want to upset anybody. The constant get-out clause in Def Leppard interviews was this determination not to offend in case it prevented them shifting units. Perhaps press, public and bands alike are all a little more relaxed about the situation now, but sixteen years ago you were supposed to fight with your label, not snuggle up to them. This total lack of revolutionary zeal and rebellious intent further disenchanted sections of the audience who saw rock'n'roll as a lifestyle aside from compromise. Joe Elliott was merely speaking the truth of course, pointing out to the fans that all bands need a good relationship with their record label, for ultimately it is in the company's hands as to whether or not a band can break through. If they choose not to push an album, not to market or advertise it appropriately, if they choose simply to sit on a record, it will not sell. Offending those who hold your livelihood in their hands is not sensible business practice and Leppard were already sound businessmen.

The real problem lay in the fact that Def Leppard did not understand the distinction between remaining 'normal blokes' and the impact of giving in to the company, a point Elliott inadvertently made obvious in speaking to *Sounds*. 'We're no different now we've got a contract. We're not on great ego trips and six buckets of heroin a day. We have people backstage to meet us – we were an hour and a half late going home last night because of the kids in the dressing room. We're still fans ourselves.' Laudable attitude though that was, it did not tackle the central problem. When Def Leppard were a bunch of lads rehearsing in Sheffield and playing the working men's clubs to subsidize their musical habit, they were free to do as they chose, an appealing image for rock fans. Now they were at the very heart of the machine, sacrificing that freedom, giving in to record company demands, all in the search for fame and fortune. Joe and the band honestly didn't see what all the fuss was about, they were merely systematically approaching their goals, making the compromises that they knew would have to be made. Their error, if error it was, was to own up to those compromises and become sullied by commerce in the process. Even if it's plainly untrue, fans like bands to operate within their own little world where such everyday considerations cannot impinge on their dreams. It's ironic that Leppard should have failed to grasp the need to build this escapist image when their songs were based wholly on mindless escapism.

The 'Hello America' debacle effectively finished Def Leppard in Britain until 'Hysteria' provided a welcome opportunity for reassessment and, complain as they might, there was little the band could do to change things. Joe tried to point out that 'people in England used to like "Hello America". We only had a negative reaction after they read the reviews, which is a shame. People should make their own minds up, not be told what to think'. Good advice, but to no avail. When *On Through the Night* was unveiled a few weeks later, the tide had turned against them, though of course matters weren't helped when people actually heard just how poor a record it was compared with the advance press that had promised a *tour de force*.

People were now confused by Def Leppard, unsure what to think of them, a confusion that extended to the press. Geoff Barton's review of the album dwelt largely on the negative side of things: 'A tiny trawler beneath a tidal wave, so swamped by the "business" . . . Producer "Colonel" Tom Allom has given the band such a smooth, sanitised sound.' It all seemed to spell doom for the band, yet Barton still gave the album four out of five, and rounded off by saying 'nevertheless, a pretty good album. Their biggest talent is their songwriting – catchy tunes abound.' Small wonder that the NWOBHM fans didn't know what to make of Leppard either. Probably the final nail in the coffin came just a couple of weeks later when Iron Maiden's eponymous debut album was released to huge acclaim. Maiden produced the kind of record that metal fans had been starved of for years – concise, aggressive, tight, no frills rock at ear-splitting volume. In contrast, *On Through the Night* looked flabby, overblown and totally lacking in impact. The chart placings told the story. *On Through the Night* reached number fifteen, *Iron Maiden* number four. Def Leppard were no longer at the top of the NWOBHM heap and the inevitable backlash was long, protracted and painful.

They had booked an extensive UK tour to coincide with *On Through the Night*, playing city halls (including Sheffield) and Odeon-sized venues all over the country, supported by the up-and-coming Magnum. Ian Ravensdale caught them for *Sounds* in Newcastle and his review was particularly perceptive: 'Even heavy metal fans must have inhibitions about letting it all rip when the kid playing the guitar looks as though he could still get half fare on the bus . . . they lack real identity and it could have been too much too soon.' Elliott was predictably upset by this blatant ageism, ranting 'young? I'm twenty-two for Chrissakes and what does it matter anyway? All this stuff about age is ridiculous. I suppose it *was* surprising when we started but time will take care of that'.

Nevertheless, it was becoming impossible to take Def Leppard seriously, they were starting to look like some sort of manufactured teenybopper band aimed directly at a heavy metal audience. Since such fans consider themselves to be outside the musical mainstream and beyond the manipulative clutches of the music business, any hint of artifice is rarely tolerated. Things simply began to get worse and worse for them, with audiences polite rather than warm in their response to the band's efforts, the hard rock lyrics sounding especially crass when coming from such an innocent-looking band.

Of course, Def Leppard had been courted so strenuously by Peter Mensch because he saw the international appeal of their music – for 'international', read 'American'. As the Def Leppard controversy raged on in the letters pages of *Sounds*, Mensch did what he really wanted to do with the band. Getting them out of the UK and off to the States, he used his contacts to organize support slots with Ted Nugent, the Scorpions and AC/DC. Each of these tours, often in enormous arenas, was tremendously successful, enabling the band to play to huge audiences in a short space of time, creating impressive word of mouth recommendations for them. They were equally popular on radio, where 'Hello America' was, unsurprisingly, in great demand. On the back of all this activity, *On Through the Night* reached a very respectable number 51 on the Billboard charts, confirming that they had made sizeable and lucrative inroads into the market that mattered most.

Their assault on the States was almost unprecedented. No British metal band had ever had such a single-minded approach to establishing itself in America before it had done so at home. Perhaps in their collective mind, they were merely distancing themselves from Britain while the storm blew itself out, hoping it would be a nine-day wonder and that they could return in triumph later in the year.

Perhaps that's so, but it's more reasonable to suggest that they had always planned this American sojourn for the summer, a time when gigs are few and far between in Britain anyway.

Some have suggested that Def Leppard took to America because they had nowhere else to turn when things were going so badly wrong at home, going on to argue that their virtual migration to the States was simply the fortunate result of circumstances beyond their control. Such comments are foolish. They had already hooked up with Mensch in the winter of 1979 and there can be little doubt that he and the band had long discussions as to how they would work the debut album, getting a foothold in certain markets around the globe. As an American, Mensch's views would not have been clouded by sentimental visions of success in the UK, a spot on *Top of the Pops* and a mention in the *Daily Mirror*. To Mensch, the UK was merely another marketplace, and a pretty insignificant one at that. For a band to earn the longevity that he was looking for, they had to be big in America, for that was the only way they could earn enough cash to keep on going. A recording, touring band is an expensive operation to maintain and it's dollars that keep the wheels turning. It may be an unpleasant fact, but fact it is. If Def Leppard wanted to see in the 1990s, they had to make it big in America. Though it would have been nice to have gone down well in the UK, ultimately it didn't really count for much, an attitude that the band took on board very quickly.

That's not to say that they always admitted to it. Joe Elliott was often extremely angry when interviewers accused him of deserting his home for America and a fat pay cheque. 'Selling out to America? That pisses me off because it's so ridiculous. We're not the first English rock band that went to the States and we won't be the last . . . America's a big market and it would be senseless to ignore it. We're out to make Def Leppard a successful band and that means going to the States. We did pretty well there too, I think we won quite a few people over. But God, we were only there a couple of months. It's not as if we went to live there.'

Just how badly Def Leppard's perceived defection had gone down was brought home to them at the Reading Festival on August Bank Holiday weekend, 1980. Leppard played on the final day, just before headliners Whitesnake were due to go on. Their absence had not made the crowd's heart grow any fonder and they were met with a fusillade of cans and plastic bottles filled with recycled waste material. Joe's memory of the show was, not surprisingly, a vivid one. 'There was just too much hard rock that weekend, there was no sort of contrast. We were one of the last bands on the bill and I reckon anyone, even the most devoted fan of that kind of music would get a bit fed up of it after three days. Probably the worst thing of all for us was having to follow Slade. They were great. They put on an amazing show and went down a storm, played the hits. It was a classic case of "follow that". We did our best but it didn't seem to go too well . . . I got a half tin of Tartan lager in my bollocks.' Unfortunately, whatever rationale the band tried to hide behind, the facts were stark. The paunchy Elliot and his comrades were now public enemy number one among the metal fraternity, treated as wimped out, sold out fakes. They were no longer welcome on British territory.

So they did what anyone sensible would do in the circumstances. They went off in search of an audience that did want them. It wasn't hard to find because they already knew where to look.

6

WAITING FOR THE MAN

The American debate is one that still rages when the conversation turns to Def Leppard. Was it mere chance that took them to America or was it their goal right from the off? Would they have inevitably appealed to an American audience in the fullness of time or was it Peter Mensch's knowledge of the market that helped steer their music in the right direction? Essentially, are Def Leppard a bona fide band of musicians or are they merely a group of chancers out to make the best and most successful career moves that they could?

The definitive answer lies in-between all those statements. More than any other NWOBHM band, perhaps more than virtually any other band in the history of British rock music, Def Leppard had a burning desire to make it big in the States. From their point of view, that was mere pragmatism, for they knew they had to make a living out of the music in order to survive. Yet Mensch's part in all of this is especially important. Although the songs on *On through the night* were removed from those of the likes of Saxon or Iron Maiden, there was very little that was star-spangled about the album. Leppard were still clearly dabbling in an age-old British hard rock tradition, in a fairly uninspired manner at that. Beneath the surface, it was clear that there were popular songwriting instincts at work, but that was a *long* way beneath.

By the time the heavy metal lynch mob got their hands on them at Reading, Def Leppard were already mutating into a very different sort of rock group, hence their poor reception. Gone were so many of the rough edges that Tom Allom had left on their album, to be replaced by a smooth confidence, a cleaner, brighter sound that lacked the grit and the grime that characterized British metal. In August 1980, Def Leppard were already starting to peddle a prototype brand of what became derisively known as 'metal lite'. Once again, musical cultures successfully blurred geographic boundaries and it was a band from Sheffield that was the instigator of one of America's most successful music forms, a style that dominated the late 1980s.

Commercially savvy, Leppard remained naive and were completely unaware of the storm they would cause just by appearing at Reading. Perhaps they were too close to the music to take an objective look at things, but it was clear to all and sundry that they were going through a rapid evolution, heading towards an end product that British fans were unwilling to accept. To argue that it was Mensch and Burnstein who guided them in this direction is putting it too strongly. What is not in question is the fact that it was they who wanted to expose Leppard to America for months at a time, drummed into them the value of that marketplace and required them to tour extensively there. Exposed to American culture on such a scale, the band couldn't help but soak it up. Joe was especially taken with FM radio, a force that was utterly reviled in the UK as the home for sanitized tosh such as Saga, Journey and Boston. Joe disagreed. 'FM radio is rock radio! It's fucking brilliant!' To hear such gushing praise about the perceived enemy could only drive further nails into Leppard's coffin at home. Within a year, they had gone from being the great white hope to utter pariahs.

From here, it was Leppard's extreme reserves of willpower and determination, coupled with some northern bloody-mindedness, that kept them going. Instead of trying to win back lost favour in the UK, they simply decided to ignore the media and continue on their chosen path. In truth, this was the turning point in their career for it meant they no longer had to pander to any stereotypes or prejudices at home, but could simply focus totally on the job in hand, cracking America.

At this stage, the Leppard organization began to shift its stance. Press comments had always been along the lines of 'heavy metal is what we love the most, we want to follow in the footsteps of Deep Purple and Led Zeppelin'. Now, although the term heavy metal was not exactly prohibited, it was a phrase to be used only with the greatest caution. Having ridden to fame on the coat-tails of the NWOBHM, for which Leppard had been very grateful at the time, Joe was now looking to put plenty of distance between his band and the rest. 'I always laugh when people accuse us of deserting the cause. Of what? What flag? Bollocks! We're nothing to do with any of you. We're nowt to do with the NWOBHM. We were always more impressed with the Rolling Stones than we were with Judas Priest.'

This is total fabrication, a reinvention to reposition them in the commercial mainstream, crucial as far as an American audience was concerned, for Mensch was planning to invest very heavily in the band's second record. If they were comparatively unimpressed with Priest, why did they choose Tom Allom to produce *On through the night*, his selection the result of an intimate knowledge of Judas Priest's *Unleashed in the east* album? The truth of the matter is that Def Leppard were defiantly heavy metal but were now changing their tune as their own tunes changed.

The crux of the matter is why did the tunes change? It's impossible to tell now whether, if Leppard had not been subjected to the reverses they suffered in England, they might have continued in a more traditional heavy metal vein or whether their musical approach would have changed as it did. Given the ambitious nature of the band, it's likely that Reading merely accelerated their drift in an American direction rather than originated it; MSB were not really replaced because they couldn't hack it in England. It was because they lacked the contacts to open up world markets. With their new management, new horizons had opened up and that was what they had always wanted.

Def Leppard have taken a great deal of flak for this over the years, but they really deserve a lot of credit for changing the way British groups looked at the world. Ordinarily, a band would never want to venture across the Atlantic until they were hugely successful at home for fear that they would be swallowed up by that vast continent and have to return home with their tails between their legs. Leppard had no such inferiority complex and felt that if you believed in what you could do and had confidence in yourselves and in your music, you could succeed anywhere. Mensch had a viable business plan using FM radio to infiltrate the market while he was also keen on the burgeoning field of the promo video. If video took off – this was several years before MTV arrived on the scene – you could appear all over the world without leaving home. They all felt that it would become incredibly important in promoting any band, knew that it would enable you to break into markets much more easily, and planned accordingly.

Without the right music though, rock bands cannot survive for long. Elliott's suggestion that the band were closer to the Stones than Judas Priest was substantially true. In effect, Leppard had lived their career in reverse, for if any part of their work had been based on compromise or could be construed as a sell out, it was the months leading up to getting their deal with Phonogram. They liked Deep Purple and Led Zeppelin it's true, but there was an equal, probably stronger love for Marc Bolan, Queen, David Bowie, Mott the Hoople and the late, lamented Mick Ronson – in *Melody Maker*'s 'Rebellious Jukebox', a kind of Desert Island Discs, Joe picked 'All the young dudes', 'Get it on,' Hunter's 'Once bitten twice shy', 'Rock'n'roll part two', Ronson's 'Angel number nine', 'John I'm only dancing', 'Won't get fooled again' and 'Sympathy for the devil' among his twelve choices, the only 'obvious' selection being Zeppelin's 'Kashmir', far too complex and atmospheric a song to be so lightly dismissed as mere metal. Def Leppard as a unit loved classic pop/rock songs, but back in 1978, it was not wise to proclaim that too loudly, Joe remarking that 'it seems to me that melody has become a foul word in England'. Songwriting was their strength and that had been compromised in the drive to earn heavy metal credentials. There was nothing necessarily wrong in that for the Police pretended to be punks to gain recognition and Elvis Costello had done the same with regard to the new wave. When you're trying to get a break, there are no rules, no principles. Once Def Leppard got the publicity they needed, they could get the deal they deserved and start to make the music they wanted to make. Def Leppard's career really began in September 1980 once the doors of the UK had closed tightly shut behind them;

the harsh facts of British life were starkly illustrated in December 1980 when they tried to play a few club dates prior to recording to rehearse new material. So badly did the tickets sell, that even some of these gigs, where they'd hoped to play to a couple of hundred fans, had to be cancelled. Goodbye Britain, hello America . . .

Def Leppard being Def Leppard, things did not go smoothly even then. It was now clear that America would become their adopted musical home for some time, but they had to accept that things would work differently there, that the music press carried far less weight than it did in the UK. Getting on to FM radio was the obvious goal for that was the best way to spread the word about the band from the east coast to the west. Where live performance had previously been of the greatest importance to them, they realized that they would have to take greater care in the studio. This caused a degree of estrangement between Pete Willis and the rest for as he pointed out in *Sounds*, 'I like the whole thing about rock bands, generally having a good laugh'. Spending months in a dingy recording environment is not the best way to getcha rocks off and it's fair to say that Willis probably viewed the prospect with less enthusiasm than the rest.

According to the rest of the group, his personality had been the most affected by their limited success. Oddly, though Elliott was the accepted frontman, the man who had to strike up a rapport with the audience, do the interviews and generally represent the group, it was Pete who was under the most pressure. A more reserved character by nature, early gigs had reputedly seen him playing guitar from the back of the stage, or even from the wings. The onset of fame and the adulation of the fans meant that he had to come to terms with being a public figure very quickly. Of the five in the band, he was the least concerned with achieving worldwide fame and so the less agreeable aspects of the job inevitably wore him down more than they did the others; the gregarious Elliott, for example, was in his element meeting, and charming, new people all the time.

Pete had an additional problem with which to deal. Short in stature, especially alongside Joe at the front of the stage, his elfin features did make him look much younger than even Rick Allen, hence the comment from Ian Ravensdale in his *Sounds* review quoted in the previous chapter. It was tough for hard bitten English crowds to warm to Willis when he looked little more than a schoolboy. Given that guitar players are often the central focus of a rock band, it was hard enough for Pete to deal with the attention, never mind the accompanying derisory comments. The fact that Steve Clark was clearly enjoying his role in it all scarcely made things any easier for him. Once on the road with a limitless supply of booze on hand, the rest of the group noticed that Pete was leaning more and more on the bottle, Elliott putting the change down to one specific incident. 'He changed on a ten hour flight. The first time we went to the States, we got on the plane at Heathrow and ten hours later Pete was carried off, bollocksed drunk. He was never the same again.'

Willis was not the only one who regularly had a few too many, for Joe later remembered seeing Clark 'puking blood back in 1978' as a result of his drinking. With another record to make though, such over-indulgence was dismissed as something that could be handled. There was no desire to throw anyone out of the band and disrupt the creative tensions that existed at such a vital stage in their career. The biggest question for now was where would they record and with whom.

Thankfully, they realized that they had made mistakes and that any blame for their British problems lay with them as much as it did the press. Elliott magnanimously accepted that 'we fell into all the traps. At the time I thought we were doing all the right things. God couldn't have told me I was wrong. Now I realize that the first album was a load of shit. It was very representative of the band for about six weeks but afterwards we weren't anything like that any more'. This time, they needed a record that they'd be able to live with indefinitely, one of which they could be proud.

Once again, Peter Mensch stepped into the breach. Even before they'd gone in to record *On through the night*, they'd had one particular producer in mind. Joe admits that 'we wanted Mutt Lange for the first one, having heard his work with City Boy, the Motors and Graham Parker. Tom Allom was the next on the list and he was great, really funny, but we didn't want to get stuck in a rut, we wanted something different, we wanted a definite improvement.' Mutt, more formally known as Robert Lange, had also produced AC/DC, rescuing their final record with Bon Scott, 1979's superb

'Highway to hell', and running the potentially difficult sessions for the follow-up, 'Back in black'. Since Mensch had worked so closely with AC/DC, he knew Lange and was instrumental in setting up the collaboration. A few more unkind critics have suggested that Lange had never previously been in the frame for the job and that it was all Mensch's doing, but Elliott's comments on bands such as the Motors ring true. Lange had compiled a diverse, idiosyncratic CV and the mix of styles which he had mastered was hugely appealing to Leppard. Free of the need to produce a metallic record, they wanted someone who could help them achieve the best possible synthesis between their pop sensibility and their avowed intention to maintain a typically British aggressive dimension to their music.

Lange was an excellent choice. With a great track record behind him, he was supremely confident in the studio and was already interested in Def Leppard. Like so many other industry insiders, he could hear the potential within the band and wanted the opportunity to help them unleash it. Sufficiently successful not to have to worry about the dictates of the record company, his very presence was enough to reassure executives that with Leppard, they were indeed on to a winner. In turn, that helped relax the band whose confidence had been dented by their British experiences. With Mutt on board, they could afford to be optimistic once again.

It's rare for Def Leppard to give birth to a record painlessly, for they appear to endure an elephantine gestation period. Preparations for their second album, a real crossroads for them, were going well. Their songwriting had improved while past studio experience had given them a better idea of what worked well on record and what did not. The body of work they had at their command this time was a considerable improvement on their first efforts and they were champing at the bit, having finished touring in September. Unfortunately, Lange was already committed elsewhere, recording Foreigner's 4, sessions which were interminable. It was not Lange's quest for perfection that held things up, but the band's own uncertainty about the material they were working on. Having planned to finish with Foreigner in October, Lange was not finally free of his commitments until May 1981. This had left Def Leppard kicking their heels for eight months.

The perceived wisdom has it that a new rock band should make a record, tour incessantly and still make its second album within a year of the first, whereupon the cycle begins anew. If the group is successful, it has to capitalize on this, strike while the iron is hot and keep the name in the forefront of people's minds. To leave the best part of two years between the first and second release is tantamount to commercial suicide. With Leppard reviled at home and virtual nobodies everywhere else, this enormous delay should really have sounded the death knell. There were many sage advisers who, by Christmas 1980, were counselling that Def Leppard needed to get an album together, and quick.

The band held their nerve, either from their own convictions or because of Mensch's glowing description of what Mutt could do for their career. Such certainty of purpose in the face of all the normal rules was proof of great collective strength of character and once more, they would be proved right. They used the down time wisely, working on their songs, adding new ones to the canon, ensuring that once they could begin work, there would be a wealth of strong material from which to choose. Revelling in the freedom they now had to explore the more melodic side of their natures, tunes aplenty came flowing from them. It's fair to say that this second record would be a far more honest representation of what Def Leppard were about and what they wanted to become.

The day of reckoning finally came in May 1981 when the band went into London's Battery Studios – Iron Maiden's customary home – to start work. Unlike the two weeks that had been lavished on *On through the night*, two full months were given to *High'n'dry*, a considerable investment of time and money and one which put the release date back still further, the album not seeing the light of day until July 1981 when it was rush-released to coincide with a previously booked touring schedule. Such indecent haste did not sit well with Lange's legendarily meticulous studio habits, but for Leppard it was a tremendous introduction to the world of professional recording. Hustled through the debut, two months seemed an eternity to them and perhaps any longer would have been too much of a culture shock. As it was, they were able to maintain their enthusiasm throughout and their obvious enjoyment of the process shone through on an album that was a 100 per cent improvement on its predecessor.

High'n'dry was no masterpiece, it's a long way from being their best work, nor will it go down in history as a turning point for popular music but for Def Leppard, it stands out as probably the most important record they've ever made. It had to show a dramatic improvement but, crucially, it needed to demonstrate a strong sense of direction, offer evidence that they had a firm hand on the tiller and that they were heading towards a definite destination. With *On through the night* widely viewed as a disappointing first blast from them, they desperately needed to silence the doubters. Amid the cries of 'sell-out', Leppard really just returned to their roots and produced a selection of driving pop rockers. The album was flawed, lacked any real dynamic range and the lyrics remained shallow and uninteresting but the sheer urgency in the playing, the absolute conviction in the delivery overshadowed these deficiencies.

It was, inevitably, Joe Elliott who put his finger on Lange's enormous contribution to Leppard's renaissance. 'Mutt works you hard. I'm a real wimp in the studio because you've got no natural adrenaline, no audience. He makes me work until it's right.' One of the most striking things about *High'n'dry* was the improvement in Joe's own voice. Even though he was still a long way from rivalling the likes of David Coverdale, he could now make the most of his still limited ability while the songs seemed to fit his range far better than previously. Joe was candid in his assessment of his own voice: 'They put up with me not being able to sing for two and a half years. My singing was absolutely useless.' No false modesty this, for any dispassionate observer would have to agree that his performance on *On through the night* was awful. True to his character though, Joe wasn't about to let a little thing like a lack of natural talent come between him and success, admitting later in *Q* that 'I'm like Kevin Keegan who wasn't as good a footballer as Glenn Hoddle, Tony Currie or Stan Bowles, but who knew that if he worked his bollocks off, he could achieve something, whereas the others were lazy . . . I'm not the most gifted – when God handed out throats, I got locked out of the room. But I was determined to do it, I would do anything . . . Mutt's really patient, he just tries to bring out in my voice what I'm capable of but what I wouldn't do myself because I'd get fed up trying. I'd pack in after six attempts but Mutt'll keep me going for twelve'. Singing on the road night after night helped him with phrasing and with pacing himself and his voice, so by the time they entered Battery Studios, Joe was something of a seasoned campaigner. Familiarity with the material helped too, but the real difference was the way in which Lange made him jump through hoops in order to get the sound right. If he failed to get it right first time, Mutt got him to record it again. And again. And again until it was exactly the way it should be. In fact, it rarely was exactly the way it should be for Joe still had much to learn about his art but Lange was experienced enough to realize when he had wrung the last ounce out of Elliott and wise enough to know when to call it a day. By the end of recording, Joe was a tired man, but a proud one too for he had proved himself a capable singer at last.

If there was a real criticism that could be levelled at him – indeed at everyone involved in the entire project – it was that they seemed determined to become the new AC/DC. Naturally Lange's involvement in *Back in Black* and *High'n'dry* meant here would be similarities in the sound, but at times, Leppard sailed a little close to the wind, with Elliott looking too keen to step into Bon Scott's shoes. With *Back in Black* such a huge hit commercially and critically, it wasn't a bad reference point and at least it proved they were heading in the right direction, for AC/DC were not a dumb metal act, but an intelligent rock band.

From the outset, it was obvious that Def Leppard demanded reassessment for the music was tighter, more dynamically structured, punchier, an altogether more arresting sound. 'Let it go' set the tone, a long way removed from the adolescent fare of 'Rock brigade'. If it was pretty standard rock'n'roll, it was done well, only diminished by the 'get ready for the back seat' sexism implicit in the lyric. Elliott apologized eight years later, saying 'I look back and think "thank God I was only twenty". I mean, the lyrics, some of them are fuckin' useless, awful "get down on your knees" stuff. Nowadays, I try to do it a bit more tactfully.'

The record carried its fair share of uncomplicated rock songs, 'High'n'dry' and 'No no no' being cases in point, the latter a classic example of heads down, see you at the end rifferama, featuring lots of senseless screaming from both Joe and the twin, inevitably duelling, guitars. 'Lady strange' also provided a flimsy excuse to cut to the guitar chase at the bridge, though the central guitar riff was worth hearing, reminiscent of Rainbow's 'Since you been gone'. Fortunately, these songs were to prove the exception rather than the rule as the group's poppier instincts tended to hold sway. 'Mirror, mirror (look into my eyes)' was a perfect example of this curate's egg of an album. Hard edged pop displaying an improvement in the songwriting, the clumsy arrangement and dubious execution meant the song sounded cluttered with little room for the instrumentation to breathe, yet it was salvaged by the layers of backing vocals which were an immensely promising departure. That careful structure was equally well employed on 'You got me runnin'', where the backing served to bolster Joe's voice which was clearly stretched by the material.

'On through the night', a hangover from the first album perhaps, let things down, for though it was obviously anthemic, deliberately, desperately so, the lyrical idea was wholly ludicrous. The concept of rock'n'roll, one of the great corporate entertainment industries, having 'no safety net' is plainly absurd while the image of Leppard as a hard living rock'n'roll band still didn't wash, especially as it looked liked they still didn't need to shave. It was a shame that the lyrics were so relentlessly crass, for musically the song was much closer to the direction Leppard were aspiring to, poppy with some very nice guitar interplay that left it rooted in the rock genre. Lyrics remained a bugbear for them, though Joe suggested that they had tried to work harder on them this time around. 'On this album, we tried to write about all sorts of stories. Steve once hijacked a taxi in Paris and tried to write a song about it, but it just sounded like a piece of shit, so we scrapped it, rewrote the lyrics and it sounded a lot better.'

The other three tracks on *High'n'dry* were especially important, each in their own distinctive fashion. Steve Clark's 'Switch 625' made it clear that here was a guitarist and writer of real distinction. Although it didn't really fit into the overall concept of the album, it demanded inclusion. The lead guitar line was excellent and the track could have been taken from the soundtrack to a European thriller. It was clear that Leppard's horizons really were broadening and 'Another hit and run' was perhaps the best example of their improved attention to detail within their songwriting. Where so much of their material was designed to rock hard, this allowed for a nice change of pace, illustrating an intuitive understanding of dynamics that would go on to serve them well in the future.

Pointing the way ahead was 'Bringing on the heartbreak' with its lovely guitar work and Gary Moore-ish introduction. 'Heartbreak' was straight out of the classic rock power ballad mould, but it took the form to a new level. It was the first really huge vocal harmony that they'd used to date, the wash of colour that would become their trademark over the years and provide the blueprint for countless imitators. Quite simply, those backing vocals were so lush, so painstakingly recorded, so awesomely bright and full of life that the sheer scope of the production was simply overwhelming, proving to be ultimately irresistible to a generation of record buyers.

With the album completed and concert dates looming, the band had little time to reflect on what they'd achieved. They could rest assured that this time around, the critics would be mightily impressed. Geoff Barton helped himself to a very large plate of humble pie in *Sounds*: 'I realize now that I wrote Def Leppard off prematurely, cruelly and unnecessarily. *High'n'dry* is a titanium toecapped kick in the teeth for Def Leppard's British critics.' The album collected the maximum five stars, but it was too little too late for the band in Britain. Minds had been made up about Def Leppard long since and though both 'Let it go' and 'Bringing on the heartbreak' were released as singles, neither charted, with the album only making number twenty-six. Elliott was philosophical about it all, accepting that 'it's irrelevant how I see things. It's how the audience sees them that decides how many records we sell. We lost our market because the music press slagged us to pieces'.

Nevertheless, the critical reappraisal was welcome, not least because Willis and the rest were becoming increasingly estranged, Willis allegedly less keen on the new direction the music was taking. Indeed there were plenty of unsubstantiated rumours in the music press that he was considering leaving the band in order to form a more traditional metal outfit. Any personal differences were buried for the course of the tour however, the band enjoying all the road had to offer. Gigs in West Germany offered some of the stranger sights as Joe recalled. 'We went to the Star Club in Hamburg in 1981 to see where the Beatles had played but it's not there any more and eventually we ended up in an underground car park which had all these women chained to the pillars and little rooms off the main area. So you'd walk around this meat market and at twenty-one it was a real eye opener. I'd never seen anything like it in Sheffield!'

With a renewed spirit of optimism spreading through the camp, even the British dates went tolerably well, although an accompanying promotional gimmick – if you took your ticket stub to the HMV chain of stores, you got 50p off the price of *High'n'dry* – tarnished things a little. Gigs just prior to Christmas 1981 proved that their rehabilitation was all but complete in the eyes of the press, though the fans still stayed away in droves. Philip Bell wrote in *Sounds* that the Leppard show was based upon 'Absolute professionalism . . . a total reassessment. It works', though *Melody Maker*'s Steve Gett was a little more circumspect in his praise, admitting that the new music was 'ideal for the US market but I have my doubts regarding the strength of their British popularity', reservations that were founded in the facts.

Although Def Leppard had had a rough time at the hands of the press in 1980, the members of the Fourth Estate could not be held solely to account for the band's failure at home. There were more fundamental, deep-seated reasons for this malaise than a simple sheaf of bad reviews. They were just the wrong band for the time. British rock music in the early 1980s was going through a conspicuously dour period with the 'indie' bands such as Joy Division, Echo and the Bunnymen and, later on the Smiths holding the more committed rock fans in thrall. If you were serious about your music, now was not the time for celebration with ever-lengthening dole queues and worsening economic situation allied to the omnipresent threat of global war as international relations reached a low point between the west and the pre-glasnost Soviet Union. What was there to celebrate?

On the other hand, on a more commercial level, it was the synthetic doodlings and fashion conscious performances of the New

Romantics that were swamping the charts. Their ethic was that things were so bad in the outside world, the only sensible response was to create your own world filled with bright and shiny young things. To gain entrance to this world of twenty-four-hour party people, you had to dress properly, drink the right cocktails and know the right people. Life could be a constant whirl if you approached it properly.

Def Leppard fell outside those two camps, too frivolous and lyrically inept for the 'indie' scene, too down to earth and 'ordinary' for the New Romantics. British music was all about image and Leppard's just did not fit in. Their only refuge would have been with the metal crowd that had initially brought them to prominence but they were set on taking revenge for Leppard's apparent betrayal of the NWOBHM and their American preoccupations. The band were even beginning to sport expensive hairdos, the Jon Bon Jovi poodle cut as it would become known later. Little wonder that Joe complained 'what we really need is an audience that'll accept a band that looks like Duran Duran but sounds like Saxon. That's the next step'. As it was, in 1981, Def Leppard were complete outcasts.

In America, things looked a lot more positive for them. With the wholesale compartmentalization of radio in the States, Leppard slotted in nicely to the FM format, all the more so now that they were working with Lange. Lange himself was the hottest name in American AOR at the time with Foreigner's *4* on its way to sales of six million units, topping the Billboard charts in the States for ten weeks. That gave Def Leppard added kudos, provided them with a way in to those radio stations which they exploited to the full. Peter Mensch had put his reputation on the line with *High'n'dry* and was determined to turn it into a major seller. In fact, it was only a minor improvement on *On through the night* in sales terms, charting at number thirty-eight, but crucially it made the breakthrough in terms of acceptance, paving the way for future triumphs.

Supporting Blackfoot, they spent much of 1981 on the road in America, playing a mix of good and bad shows, Elliott accepting that 'other bands have time to evolve and grow up in the small clubs. We're making all our mistakes in front of thousands of people'.

Mistakes or not, they were beginning to make waves in America and were able to live the life of bona fide rock stars as Elliott remembers. 'We had little girls chasing us all over the place, everywhere we went it was summer, we'd be round the pool all day and doing a couple of interviews. Pete was living the lifestyle and putting less and less into the performance. The rest of us were pretty rampant in those days and we'd all indulge in a drink or birds if they were around, but it was always "enough's enough, we've got a gig tomorrow". Pete got his comeuppance though – we used to gaffa tape his boots to the roof of the van and when he was asleep we'd put shaving foam on the back of his hand and tickle his nose with a feather.'

Such games helped relieve the tension in the rest of the camp but did little for Willis's peace of mind. It was beginning to become obvious that he might yet go the way of MSB. Ironically, they were still giving the band pause for thought more than a year after their demise. Elliott was especially angry with the way things had worked out. 'It cost us a fortune to get rid of them. They're getting points off *High'n'dry* for as long as it sells. If say, 10,000 copies sell in ten years' time, they'll get money off it. They had nothing to do with this album. They were with us when we did the first so maybe they're entitled to a little bit of that, because they did get us a deal with Phonogram but they're entitled to nothing off this second one as far as I'm concerned.'

Such businesslike preoccupation with the pennies might have served the band well in their commercial dealings, but it did little for the public's perception of them, notably in England. Elliott's attitude seemed churlish to say the least given that Leppard were starting to look like a real act for the future. Like it or not, MSB had arranged their deal with Phonogram and if they hadn't done so, who's to say that Leppard might not have still been languishing in obscurity? It was the very fact that they had a deal that enabled them to go on to make a second record and it doesn't seem especially unfair that MSB should be entitled to some of the financial rewards for the hard work they put in. It's one thing managing a band that's already got a deal and a reputation, it's quite another to take one from the clubs and win them a record contract.

These outbursts could only add to the impression that Leppard were a bunch of money grabbing thugs and it detracted from the great strides they'd made on record. Rightly or wrongly, money seemed to be central to every move that the group made and with a skilled negotiator like Mensch behind them, they generally got the best deals. Def Leppard could not complain if people thought they were tailoring their sound to earn the maximum amount of money, for money seemed to be their greatest preoccupation.

Their bluff, blunt Yorkshire manner got them into trouble on many occasions for bands are not really supposed to speak the truth when it comes to hard cash. When you then attack the press's favourite band at the same time, you're just asking for trouble, so that's what Joe did. 'The Clash, they're middle class. They're making money but they're embarrassed by it.' Leppard were never embarrassed by their ability to make money. It was that that had allowed them to escape lives in the factories of Sheffield and had freed them to see the world. As one of the great working class escape routes – football's the other one in Britain – one of the biggest reasons for joining a rock band was to get rich. Why be embarrassed about it? The answer was that in Britain, flaunting it was not the done thing, screaming 'loadsamoney' in 1981 was not as acceptable as it became in the late eighties. It was chic to be poor, or at least to pretend to be poor.

America suffers from no such inhibitions. The American Dream itself is based on success, the nation prides itself on its egalitarian way of life. If you have the talent and the drive to get ahead, then you can, or so the story goes. If you do make it big, you should be proud of your hard work, pleased that you finally made it and revel in your self-created wealth. If money's not there to be enjoyed, what is it for? Nor were the nation's doors closed to those from abroad who might add something to the culture as Def Leppard clearly did, even though some might sneeringly suggest that that says more about the paucity of American culture than the quality of Leppard's music. Never mind, America was happy to lavish its dollars on Def Leppard and the band were happy to reciprocate by giving them what they wanted – a damn fine evening out and a record that they could enjoy over and over again. For those who liked their rock music clean and simple, Leppard were the perfect soundtrack to the perpetual party that accompanied the Reagan years as a nation fell in love with itself all over again. If the band stood out like a sore thumb in Britain, America provided ample recompense, taking Leppard to its heart. It was a love affair that had only just begun.

7

FIREPROOF

One thing about success: it keeps you busy. Touring constantly through to December, the band wanted to take a brief sabbatical at the start of 1982 in order to prepare material for their new record. They took heart from the warm reception they'd received in the States and the gradually increasing media profile they'd earned for themselves there, while their European following had been enhanced by a tour supporting Judas Priest. Having made an artistic breakthrough with *High'n'dry*, they were determined to use the platform they'd built for themselves, taking their music on to the next level. With two albums under their belt, they had a pretty good idea how the studio worked and were starting to realize that perhaps the available technology was not being fully utilized by a range of artists whose minds were still rooted in 1970s methodology. With new inventions and innovations constantly coming on stream, it was time that somebody turned recording on its head, dispensed with the conventions and approached making a record in a spirit of iconoclastic fervour. One member of the band remarked that 'we wanted to make "Star Wars" for the ears'.

The author of that remark was Phil Collen. He'd been brought into the group during the recording of their third album, *Pyromania*, to replace Pete Willis. By the time they convened at Battle's Park Gate studios to work on the basic tracks for the album, it was becoming increasingly obvious that Willis was out of step with the other four. Musically things were still reasonably okay, with Pete co-writing four songs from the album. The problems were on a personal level, for while Steve Clark was still drinking heavily, it had made little difference to his personality, nor his ability to work. For Pete Willis, drink had, according to the others, changed a lot of things. Joe Elliott's version of events was stark. 'He was fired because he was an arsehole when he was drunk. He suffered from the classic Little Man syndrome; five feet two, has a pint and all of a sudden he's eight foot nine. He was a nasty guy to be around when he was drunk.' Not only did Willis give Leppard trouble, he began to argue with Lange about the actual recording methods used on *Pyromania*. Since Lange was at the pinnacle of his profession, this was not the most intelligent of moves. As the sessions wore on, Pete's presence became increasingly disruptive, to the point where the band ordered Peter Mensch to get rid of him.

To his credit, Mensch told them where to get off. While cowardly bands habitually hide behind managers, forcing them to do their dirty work because they're ultimately just paid employees, Mensch wasn't going to let them dodge their obligations so easily. He did not believe it was his place to sack Pete, especially since the decision was based on musical grounds, given Pete's poor studio attitude. More importantly, he felt it was right that Willis should hear it from the men who wanted shot of him, felt that after all his efforts, he deserved more than just receiving his cards in the post. Summoning up the courage to do the deed, Willis was officially made an ex-Leppard at the start of July 1982.

Paradoxically, *Pyromania* contained some of Willis's best moments, for he did contribute distinctive guitar work to all the backing tracks before his departure. As a writer too, he could feel justifiably happy with songs like 'Comin' under fire', 'Billy's got a gun' and, in particular, the excellent 'Photograph'. While he was able to produce work of that calibre, it's amazing that Def Leppard could not find some way to accommodate him within the line-up. After all, they'd tolerated Joe Elliott's inadequate voice for a couple of years, so why not keep Pete at arm's length, but still involved as a writer and studio performer?

Much of the answer lies in that nebulous quality 'chemistry'. When Def Leppard were five likely lads back in Sheffield, fuelled by the

Above: All the young dudes – Rick, Phil, Sav, Steve, and Joe, 1983.

Left: Leppard conquer America, 1983.

White lightening – Steve Clark.

A band that looks like Saxon and sounds like Duran Duran.

Rick Savage, "Adrenalize".

Joe Elliot tears it down.

Sav, Viv, Joe, Rick, and Phil prepare to get rocked, 1992.

Above: Phil with Brian May at the Mercury tribute, April 1992.

Right: Joe Elliot and his hysterical trousers.

Back in black, 1992.

Above: Jon Bon Jovi keeps an eye on the competition; Viv, Sav, Rick and Joe on the "Vault" promo tour 1995.

Left: Rick Allen and real drums, 1995.

Joe Elliott, Spain, 1995.

musketorial principle of 'all for one and one for all', the band had that indefinable something, a common goal that drove them on. Somewhere along the way, Pete had mislaid that original intensity and was channelling his energies in different directions. As the band had no patience with slackers, he was already on decidedly dodgy ground. Breaking point came when he and the band fell out with one another and ceased to be on friendly terms. Rock bands are a very peculiar social grouping, unlike any other work group that you could encounter. In the office, factory or sports field, managers compile a team made up of the most talented people they can attract given their location, their wage structure and so on. A rock group is much more like a social club where the level of your ability is often far less important than whether or not you're on good terms with your band mates.

There are good operational reasons for this, since touring groups tend to live in and out of one another's pockets for months at a stretch and, if there's any animosity between the individuals, a gruelling itinerary can quickly degenerate into an absolute nightmare. More than that though, a rock group is often ruled by the gang mentality that carries kids through their school years. It becomes a self-sufficient pack that scorns the outside world, has its own jokes, its own way of working, its own way of life. Everyone knows what makes the others tick, there are precious few secrets from one another and intruders are definitely not welcome. More than anything else, life in a band has to be fun because otherwise it's just another job, the very routine that people run away to the rock'n'roll circus to avoid in the first place.

It's only natural that musicians cultivate different friendships away from their own band, people they can spend time with when they're not working or other musos who they've encountered on the road and who understand the peculiar demands placed on them. One such musician, a guitarist, who'd entered Def Leppard's circle was Phil Collen, from Walthamstow. Born in December 1957, he'd received his first guitar as a birthday present in 1973. By the end of the decade, he was a leading light with glam-rockers Girl, a group that had always threatened to become big, yet had never quite managed to make the breakthrough. Viewed as too gimmicky by some because of their androgynous behaviour, their similarity to the New York Dolls and their garish make-up, they were trying to keep alive a form that had already slipped into the twilight world of nostalgia – if people wanted to hear any glam rock, Gary Glitter, Slade and the Sweet were still knocking around the cabaret circuit, so a new band in the same vein was virtually redundant.

In the early months of 1982, Girl had finally been forced to accept the inevitable and had disbanded, leaving Collen without a job. News of his unemployment soon reached Leppard's ears and while Pete Willis was being ushered out of the front door, Collen nipped in through the back to take his place. No-one could question his ability as a guitarist, for technically he was quite superb with an added depth to his playing that Willis, and for that matter, Clark sometimes lacked. How strange then that such a gifted player should come on to the market at the exact moment when Def Leppard needed a new guitarist. Synchronicity is indeed a wonderful thing.

Where some see lucky coincidence, others sense darker forces at work. As a band committed to their career, Def Leppard were not men who were keen on taking needless risks. Willis had become something of a liability and, if Leppard were to make the final push towards superstardom, they had to be able to rely on every piece of the machine doing its job at all times. If *High'n'dry* hadn't brought quite the return that Mensch's investment warranted, he was not dismayed, remaining confident that their time would come. Searching his own conscience in order to decide whether he had done all he could, he decided that the overall outlay on *Pyromania* should be doubled to make absolutely sure that there was not a single prospective record buyer that did not know all there was to know about this record. If you're pushing the boat out that far, you have to make really sure there are no holes in the bottom. Willis looked like a potential leak, so his dismissal must have been on Mensch's mind, the more so since stories emanating from the Leppard camp suggested that his drinking was slowing things down so badly it was costing them up to £10,000 a week in lost time at a point where the group was already half a million in debt.

As a conscientious and thoroughly professional manager though, he accepted that it was not his place to change the group's personnel and so he kept his own counsel. However, he was also known to be a keen admirer of Phil Collen's and one is left to wonder whether his name might have occasionally cropped up in conversation, the more so as Girl were disintegrating.

The principal players would strenuously deny it, but one can't help but feel that had Girl been going from strength to strength and had Phil not suddenly become available, Pete Willis would have completed work on *Pyromania* and joined the band for their global trek. For a band that likes to eliminate risks and play the percentages, sacking a founder member midway through making the album they hoped would make their fortunes would have been unthinkable; they might have been unable to find a suitable replacement, the chemistry with some unknown new boy might not have worked, the whole balance of the band might have been fatally disrupted. That's just not their style.

The official version of events says that Willis's conduct was beyond redemption, yet accounts from the group say that the problems with him were at their worst on the road. If that was the case, the time to sack him would have been at the end of the 1981 tour or, if they wanted to give him time to sort himself out, right at the beginning of the *Pyromania* sessions if he hadn't shaped up. If he really had been as incapable of working as they suggest, how was he able to co-write four songs? Certainly, if Willis had become so problematical, why would they have even allowed him to start working on the album, for the traumas clearly pre-dated the recording of *Pyromania*? He did survive four months' worth of work on it after all, not a course of events that implies total dissatisfaction with his contribution, or complete ineptitude on his part. The facts suggest that the band wanted Pete out, that he was drinking too heavily, but that they didn't want to take the risk of sacking him without having a replacement in mind. Girl's dissolution solved all their problems.

Lange was especially pleased with this development, for he was impressed by Collen's ability and with his willingness to work hard in the studio. For Phil, the opportunity in Leppard was too good to let slip for as he admitted 'Girl had finally split, I was almost penniless. I got a call out of the blue from Joe asking me to take over from Pete Willis and I was so content just to be back in a band again'.

Collen's involvement with *Pyromania* began in July as the group moved from Park Gate to the more familiar environment of Battery Studios in London to begin overdubbing. With all the basic tracks down, it was here that Lange's expertise was especially important, for it was here that the new Def Leppard sound was really constructed. For a further five months, every note, every line was considered, reconsidered, reworked and refined. The vast swathes of sound that had so distinguished songs like 'Bringing on the heartbreak' on *High'n'dry* were deployed once again, but this time with yet greater style and conviction. The culmination of this huge physical and mental effort was a record the like of which, from a sonic standpoint at least, had not been heard before.

Never ones to hide their light under a bushel, Leppard were forgivably bullish about their new product. Joe's objective opinion being that 'I seriously think *Pyromania* is one of the best recorded LPs I've ever heard. Like Queen had done ten years earlier, we rewrote the rule book on how to make rock music in 1983 with *Pyromania*. We knew there had to be a better way'. Joe in particular had reason to applaud the results, for his voice continued to improve at an alarming rate. Lange's quest for perfection had clearly brought things out that he didn't believe he had in him, but it was not without a price. For several weeks, Elliott's voice simply packed up under the strain and it wasn't until after he'd flown to see a specalist in New York that he was able to complete work on the album. The effort had to be worth it though, for now the last impediment to Leppard's success had been removed. If Joe's rasping vocals had put off likely buyers in the past, those punters could find no such reasons to leave *Pyromania* on the racks. Buttressed by those trademark backing vocals, Joe Elliott now possessed a fine rock'n'roll larynx with an impressive range to boot.

With the musical obstacles removed, it was left to Mensch to take care of business and make sure that all the promotional tools were in place. While the band had been recording for nine months, he and Burnstein had not been idle, putting in an equally awesome number of hours on the commercial side of things. Record pluggers were briefed, Phonogram alerted to the quality and ground-breaking nature of the album, video directors approached with a view to getting clips on the imminent MTV cable channel, local radio stations across the States plied with promotional items leading up to the release of the album. Everything was in hand, planned with the same attention to detail that Lange applied to his production duties. They had not recouped the sizeable sum they had pumped into *High'n'dry* and were determined to make sure that the same did not happen again.

With such powerful personalities as Mensch and Lange on the team, there were suggestions that Leppard were little more than puppets, dancing to their tune, fronting an enormous organization. It was an accusation that rankled, with Steve Clark especially vociferous in his attempts to put the record straight.

'*Pyromania* is a great record. We had a fair idea that the material we had prepared was strong enough to beat *High'n'dry* but to be honest it came as a real shock to find us top three in America all through the summer. We spent nine months on and off doing the album and getting everything exactly right, including the business side of things, so we did have everything geared up for its release. It was in the top ten in America before we'd even promoted it! We did go for this one correctly right from the word go but no matter how long we spent getting the production right, you can't deny the fact that they are, in one way or another, all great tunes. It wasn't a clear-cut attempt at turning us into the biggest thing since sliced bread.'

The songs were undeniably strong, certainly the best body of work they'd yet produced, but the plain truth was that it was the level of production that propelled *Pyromania* into the history books. What is overlooked is the fact that Def Leppard were very much part of that production; they had written the basic songs, they contributed ideas in the studio, ideas which Lange's know-how turned into reality. The whole process was a team effort as most of the great albums are.

Oddly though, probably the most astounding thing about *Pyromania* was that in many ways, it didn't sound like a record that had taken the best part of a year to create. When an artist is in the studio for such a prolonged period, the results are often horribly laboured, lacking in excitement or a spark of life, removed totally from the real world. *Pyromania* did not smack of self-indulgence, for the highly original, if rather bombastic, sound aside, it was a model of economy in many ways. As far as the basics went, everything had been pared right back to the minimum, removing the over-playing that had so cluttered the previous albums. The extensive preparation time they'd allowed themselves was not wasted either, for the early months of 1982 had seen them honing every song, cutting away the excesses, leaving just the kernel of the original idea. In turn, that opened up the spaces for embellishment with those dripping, over the top harmonies to take centre stage, not unlike the cod-operatic structures used on Meat Loaf's *Bat out of hell*. A greater compliment yet and one which the band would settle for, was that *Pyromania* had the stamp of classic Queen about it, the epic dynamics of 'A night at the opera', the joyous exuberance of 'A day at the races'. Love it or loathe it, driving rock music, played well and played confidently can carry all before it, sweeping up die-hard opponents in its wake. This was the goal that Leppard wanted to attain.

Part of the allure was that, again like Queen in their heyday, Leppard weren't afraid to inject a little humour into their songs, even if it was in the form of dumb studio in-jokes such as 'Rock of ages'. It succeeded in lightening the tone as Joe explained: 'We wanted to bring a little bit of fun back into it, put our tongues in our cheeks slightly. I just got the feeling that things were becoming too po-faced, too serious – you can't entertain people unless you're enjoying what you're doing yourself. I don't want to prowl around the stage all stern and grim-faced.' Small wonder that he was moved to add 'I'd say Iron Maiden, Saxon and ourselves are the Sweet of today! There are definite comparisons'. 'Rock of ages' was crammed full of rock'n'roll clichés, it read like a Gary Glitter tribute, a mindless stomp that was good fun, but very much apart from the rest of the music which was determined to make its mark.

From the very first chords on the album, it was apparent that something had changed, drastically and for the better. The atmosphere and the scale that leapt out of the grooves gave early warning that Def Leppard had taken a quantum leap into the unknown and had benefited from the experience. Almost a decade and a half later the chiming guitars, the shining vocals, the crashing drums all sound a little old hat for they've been so regularly and so slavishly copied, but in February 1983 such clarity of sound was highly unusual. *Pyromania* was light years ahead of *On through the night* and it was hard to credit that the same band had made both recordings. Even Joe was surprised by the distance they'd travelled in so short a space of time. 'If you listen to our first album and then our third and you can't tell the difference, then you shouldn't be listening to hard rock music anyway. We're performing the songs better. We're writing better songs. The production's better. We've got more experience . . . we have never tailored our music for the radio, things just change, they move on.'

Even so, radio was attracted to the new Def Leppard simply because the new Def Leppard was more attractive. With all extraneous material chopped away, the melodies were clearer, the tunes easier to follow, the choruses more memorable. 'Comin' under fire' was a case in point for it centred around the very simplest of guitar riffs which ushered the song into a massive chorus, Joe adding probably his best vocal performance to date to crown a track that no other member of the NWOBHM could ever have performed. The school of 1979 was now but a fading memory, though a few traces remained, notably amid the atrocious quality of the lyrics. 'Rock! rock! (till you drop)' was a case in point where the crystal clear production had to do battle with the sort of sexist rubbish that was continuing to give rock a bad name. The idea that women were there to entertain the likes of Mr Elliott was Neanderthal in the extreme, though the lyrical thrust was, fortunately, largely lost beneath the huge wall of sound. Bon Scott could get away with these lyrics, but they should have died with him in 1980. Joe suggested that 'I don't honestly believe anybody takes them seriously or takes any real notice of them. They're either completely abysmal or absolutely brilliant'. No prizes for guessing which.

'Stagefright' would not win any prizes for intellectual enlightenment either, Joe informing the world that 'it's about women who come backstage after shows. They show you their wares and then when you take them as far as they want to go, they don't wanna know any more. It happens all the time'. If this was a plea for sympathy with the star's plight, it fell on deaf ears, overshadowed again by the musical accompaniment which defied criticism. Those backing vocals stole the show once more, laying down the plans that Bon Jovi would later expand upon, notably on 'Slippery when wet'. The rhythm section was tight and powerful, providing the basis for a superb guitar solo, much the best that Leppard had so far recorded.

Where Leppard really had learned their craft was in the pacing of the set. To make a record stand out from the crowd of releases, it needs to be something of an event, it needs something that is original or idiosyncratic. With songs like 'Die hard the hunter', they provided it, the whirling sound effects offering something different from the competition, the bluesy introduction adding another element to the sound mix, the middle section all the more aggressive and potent in contrast. 'Billy's got a gun' was obviously in the same mould, building slowly into an epic from a brooding, 'Kashmir' opening. Clearly, songs like this were Leppard's stab at achieving the legendary status they coveted, tackling bigger lyrical subject matter, handling more complex atmospheres. Sensibly, they chose not to insist on using the wide screen on every song and were happy to loosen things up on 'Foolin'', its delicacy of touch and intimate introduction offering brief respite from the emotional clout of 'Die hard the hunter'. In the same fashion, the run off groove at the end of side two was filled with industrial noise, akin to something that U2 might have put on *Zooropa* a decade later.

Though Def Leppard may have dreamed of replacing Led Zeppelin via such songs as 'Billy's got a gun', it was clearly elsewhere that their real talents lay. As a band they were at their best when delivering classic hard edged pop as Mott the Hoople or Slade had done before them. 'Action, not words' was a lovely example of the genre, very light, very poppy, very enjoyable, memorably coloured by the most attractive guitar figure. If that was good, 'Photograph' was peerless, commercial mainstream pop at its sublime best, lyrically intriguing, based on an obsessive fascination with Marilyn Monroe. Huge drums, chugging rhythm, a sumptuous, warm guitar line crowning a gorgeous chorus, it was an obvious hit with 'Top Ten' written all over it. It said much for the way that Leppard were treated in the UK that it only reached number 66 when, the following year, Van Halen cloned 'Photograph' and the resulting 'Jump' single spent weeks on the survey, peaking at number seven.

That was the great problem that Leppard still had to overcome, for while they were producing the very best of straightforward classic American rock, their home audience only wanted to hear that kind of song from real Americans. No amount of persuasion could, at this stage, persuade them otherwise. To be fair, the press realized just how good Leppard now were. In his rave four star review in *Sounds* (oddly the same rating as *On through the night*, one less than *High'n'dry*), Geoff Barton made it clear that this was their finest moment: '[I'm] astonished by the Def ones new found maturity, reeling from the soaring grandeur of the song arrangements, awe-struck by the sheer brooding atmospherics of Mutt Lange's masterful production . . . I'm with Def Leppard every stratospheric centimetre of their riotous rock'n'roll re-entry.'

Melody Maker's Nick Kemp, not a renowned supporter of Leppard in the past, ventured to the Marquee to catch their first date, fitted in to the itinerary to give Phil Collen a chance to debut live out of the full glare of the spotlight. Kemp's analysis was apposite, noting that it 'proved Collen's worth to the band. He's given them the maturity they've always lacked . . . "Photograph" is a pop-rocker that ought to take the charts by storm.' His view of Collen was unerringly accurate. An unashamed fan of glam, his bright yet economic guitar style did add a new dimension to the sound, but it was his perspective on the group as an outsider that was so very valuable. For four years, the Def Leppard line-up had remained intact, all five musicians having been together from a time way before their first ever gig. It's an old truism, but they were simply too close to the band to be properly objective about what they were doing. While outside influences like Lange and Mensch were helpful, even they could never be part of the inner sanctum, the Leppard think-tank. Only those five knew what it was like to be on stage together, to write and perform together as a unit. Bringing in Collen was a breath of fresh air, a catalyst that made them question every aspect of the band, re-evaluate all that they were doing, all the habits they'd fallen into. Collen injected new impetus into things, able also to offer wise counsel about the way promising groups could fail to fulfil their potential. Helping steer them away from the traps was as much a part of Collen's input as his unquestionable skill as writer and player.

UK gigs followed hard on the heels of the release of *Pyromania*. This could be seen as loyalty to the old home, giving them the first chance to see the show, but it was more likely another piece of shrewd business planning. Sensing that *Pyromania* would fare little better than *High'n'dry*, it was good commercial sense to use the UK as a warm-up for the real tests that were to come on the arena stages in America. At the same time, delaying their arrival in America would give the promotional machine the time to build the album into the monster success everybody wanted and expected. Leppard could then jet into the States like conquering heroes. It was a strategy that worked to perfection, *Pyromania* reaching the Top Ten on the Billboard survey before the band had played a gig in support of it.

Not that the UK gigs were treated lightly, for as Joe made clear, 'deep down, we'd love to be big in Britain. I'd forsake being able to walk down Oxford Street for succcess in England any day'. It remained a sizeable priority for them but it still proved an impossible nut to crack, *Pyromania* edging up to number eighteen in the album chart. As a consequence, they were only able to play eleven UK dates through February and March with Rock Goddess in support. They were still stuck on the Odeon circuit, with venues ranging between 1500 and 3000 seats in size. Despite their global success, things still hadn't changed when they returned for a few Christmas shows. Simon Scott reviewed the Birmingham Odeon gig, damning them with faint praise: 'On stage, Def Leppard bring another dimension that their recorded work merely hints at.'

Joe candidly admitted that financially at least, they were on to a loser. 'People haven't got the dough to see bands like us out of interest like they used to in the old days. They save their money for the big tours like AC/DC or Queen. The reality is that America's paying for us not to be big in Britain at the moment . . . we're losing a heckuva lot of money here. We're going to lose £50,000 just by playing eleven gigs. It's ridiculous. If we were only in it for the money like some people think, then faced with that kind of financial disaster, we'd say "No way!" We wouldn't play one gig here and we'd be £50,000 better off, that's £10,000 each . . . at this moment, we're still in debt, though obviously that situation's changing rapidly.' Though Elliott was merely trying to inform their UK fans, trying to help them understand their situation, explaining that they were not rolling in it, such comments had the opposite effect, making him appear more and more like an accountant, a singer who went on stage with a calculator and a till roll so that during the instrumental breaks he could tot up the evening's receipts.

Such an attitude was a total irrelevance in the States where only the quality of the music was an issue, for it was a given that you would want to make money out of your talents. With the added impetus given to *Pyromania* by their extensive touring schedule, it spent most of the summer in the top three, including two weeks at number two behind Michael Jackson's *Thriller*. Success doesn't come much bigger. In a recession hit market – AOR heavyweights Asia had been forced to cancel shows because of the economic downturn and the consequently depressed market – Leppard proved to be fireproof, 'recession-proof' as Elliott termed it.

They were the hottest ticket wherever they went, playing to packed auditoriums of 10,000, 15,000, 20,000 or more. Ultimately, *Pyromania* clocked up ninety-two straight weeks on the Billboard chart and six million album sales in the US alone, 9.4 million worldwide, firmly establishing it as one of *the* landmark rock recordings. Collen put his finger on the key to Leppard's success – they offered people something they couldn't get elsewhere: 'There was a huge great gap between REO Speedwagon and Van Halen and we just happened to fit that area perfectly.' Nothing machiavellian in that, it was simply that many saw the hard rock bands as too loud or too simplistic or their audience as too threatening to get involved with while at the other end of the spectrum, American soft rock was simply too soporific for rock'n'roll fans to bear.

Girls made up much of the first group, their boyfriends the second category. What Def Leppard provided was a band that they could enjoy unconditionally, giving couples a shared interest while singles, male or female, had a band they could enjoy with their friends. In marketing, it's down to a knowledge of demographics and for Leppard, those demographics stacked up just perfectly. It's a remarkable thing, but hard rock had long since prided itself in being an all-male preserve, excluding girls except in the role of groupies. Leppard's lyrics were little better than that while some of Joe's comments on the fairer sex were hardly couched in the most seductive of language: 'Rule One – don't lose your hardcore fans. You can end up with a ninety-five per cent female audience who you know aren't going to be there next year unless you put out another hit single.'

Nevertheless, to the industry's movers and shakers such as Mensch, getting girls to the gigs and to buy the records was a sensible move. Why restrict yourself to fifty per cent of the possible audience when you can appeal to everyone? A few rock groups such as Queen and Thin Lizzy, trading on Phil Lynott's roguish charm, had managed to bring a greater proportion of girls to the concert hall, but with most rock bands, concert-going was still a prospect that could fill the strongest stomach with foreboding. Leppard turned gigs into celebratory occasions, welcoming everyone in for a huge party. Suddenly girls started to buy their records in real quantities too which had an enormous impact on their sales.

For the boys, there are times when you want something a little easier on the ears than Led Zeppelin, something that is simple verse chorus, verse chorus, something you can sing along to enjoy without having your ears bleed from the effort. Def Leppard's metal lite was the perfect way to wind down and relax, or prepare yourself for an evening with Ted Nugent. There was no stigma attached to listening to *Pyromania* as there was if you admitted to a penchant for Saga or Toto. Leppard were still a band with an edge.

These were developments that plainly perplexed Elliott as he frankly confessed in the late eighties. 'We've managed to get away with murder on the cross-over factor. We're got just ugly enough faces not to worry the lads and in America, we still get kids in Metallica T-shirts at our gigs. Bon Jovi don't get that. We get Vietnam vets who stand unembarrassed next to a sixteen year-old girl that's wetting her knickers.' Inelegantly and unchivalrously put, but true nonetheless. Def Leppard blazed a trail that had seemingly never occurred to anyone else and changed the face of rock marketing in the process. This may not have been as important to the fans or critics as a musical breakthrough such as *Revolver* or *The Velvet Underground & Nico*, but for the industry as a whole, it opened up new vistas that helped transform rock'n'roll into the avowedly corporate institution it is today.

Not that the band were shy of the corporate implications of their work. They were willing to co-operate with their record company to an unprecedented extent. That earned plenty of cynical criticism, with Leppard portrayed as a band that would roll over at the sight of a dollar sign, but in reality, it was simple common sense of the sort they'd employed right from the off. If you want the company to work for you, you have to work for the company as Joe explained. 'It is a machine and I see it first hand. We're one of the few that actually put up with anything they want us to do because we feel we need to. In the States, you get up and you do some phone interviews, travel by bus or plane to the venue and then maybe two or three of us will go to the radio stations. About eight, we have the "meet and greet" where you put on your smiley face, do photos and autographs for a while. Then it's off to the venue and I can have maybe thirty or forty-five minutes to myself before we go on stage. Sometimes we might have to do the "meet and greet" after the show or do a late night radio interview too.'

The most bizarre manifestation of Def Leppard's incredible love affair with the American people came in their stage wear. Rejected by Britain, they took solace, or revenge, in sporting Union Jack T-shirts and shorts. Within weeks, this spawned copycat dressing amongst their ardent fans and then a new line in merchandise. When the touring finally came to a halt late in the year, the massed ranks of American youth were awash with the Union flag that their forebears had fought so hard to have removed from their soil 200 years previously! By the end of 1983 with a solid year of touring behind them, the American Music Awards, voted for by the public, underlined Leppard's pre-eminence and the value of such a strong work ethic. When the votes were counted, they won awards as Top Group, Top Live Act, Top LP, Top LP Sleeve, Best Male Singer, Top Male Sex Object (Elliott), second best tour. Where do you go from there? According to Steve Clark 'there's still room for lots of improvement. We're not going to repeat the formula. Phil's contributing much more in the writing department and we've got some great ideas. Some will be quite adventurous and some will be in the typical Leppard tradition. We're more concerned with developing our potential than cloning our past.' Though they were on top of the world as 1983 came to a close, it would be close to four years before that next recording would be released. By then, the pressures of following up a hit would seem irrelevant. Real life would come crashing down on the kings of good time rock'n'roll.

8

ANIMAL MAGIC

Standard music business lore has it that once you've made an exceptionally successful album, you should flog it to death on the road, check straight into a studio and repeat the whole process within twelve months. Otherwise, the audience with its legendary minute attention span will have moved on to something else. Fortunately, many artists have a rather higher opinion of their fans than the executives do, Def Leppard being one such band. Sensibly, they felt that if nine million people had bought *Pyromania* and loved it, they'd be happy to buy the next one, whenever it was out, providing it measured up to the same standards. There again, leaving it four years was pushing the public's patience to extremes . . .

It should have all been so straightforward really. The progression from *High'n'dry* to *Pyromania* showed that they were on the top of their form and the partnership with Mutt Lange seemed to have plenty left in it. During a well deserved break after taking *Pyromania* to the world, the band settled down to pre-production in Dublin. They had taken a house there once the tour had ended in February 1984, another controversial move that merely enhanced their reputation for looking after the pennies as Joe explained: 'The government got more money – a lot more money – than we did for *Pyromania* and we just didn't agree with that.' Hence they opted for tax exile in a country that is famed for its relaxed attitude towards artists of every kind. By now, none of the band were resident in England, though how they reconciled that position with Rick

Savage's views on home was not recorded: 'We have a responsibility to English people – to everybody who likes you – but especially to the English first and foremost because we are English.' Not a responsibility that extended to swelling the coffers of the Exchequer that paid out the dole money to some of their fans though.

Naiveté aside, Dublin provided an excellent base from which to work, the recording and rehearsal facilities expanding rapidly there as a new musical infrastructure grew up around the success of U2. Having written material both separately and together, the plan was to get together in August with Mutt, listen to all the tapes and select the best material for further work at the studio they'd booked in Hilversum, Holland. Very quickly, those crucial early days degenerated into disaster as it became apparent to one and all that Mutt Lange was in no fit state to continue working with them. Having followed Foreigner's *4* with *High'n'dry* and then *Pyromania*, he had become embroiled in another mammoth project, producing *Heartbreak city* for the Cars.

His almost insane drive for perfection meant that all the time he was working, Lange was under the most intense pressure, always looking for the tiniest detail that might be letting down a song. Such an obsessive quest had to take a toll on his nerves and by the time he reached Dublin, he was already in a state of virtual collapse. As Joe recalled, 'Mutt dropped the bombshell that he couldn't do the album. The Cars' album really took a lot out of him and he said he wasn't ready to spend another year in the studio'. Bombshell was the right word for having to embark on such an important album project without their mentor at the recording console was a daunting prospect. Clearly Def Leppard were not Lange's pet studio project, for if they had not been good songwriters and strong performers, he would have had no raw material with which to work. Nevertheless, the band had to concede that Mutt had been an essential ingredient in their meteoric rise over the previous three years. Rick Savage was quick to accept that, saying 'Mutt is one of the main reasons that Def Leppard are successful, he's a great producer and I don't think anybody in their right mind should turn him down. He is a perfectionist and that's why his records sound so good.'

How had Lange come to be such an important member of the

team? In the recording process, one should never under-estimate the value of another – highly skilled – pair of ears from outside the group, particularly if a band is still in its relative infancy and is consequently unfamiliar with the recording process. If you've written a song, the natural inclination is to treat it like your own child, to believe that it is the greatest four minutes' worth of music ever heard and that it will spend months atop the charts and years in people's hearts. Obviously the truth is often very different – the track may be too long, the bridge may be too derivative, the melody might lack a little punch, the guitar solo could be too indulgent. One of Lange's greatest gifts was to break each and every song into its smallest constituent parts, examine them and then piece it back together. Such a task requires a phenomenal memory as well as an absolute understanding of each song, so it's little wonder that Lange's work was so exhausting. Joe compared it with the production of a feature film, each piece put together in isolation to the rest so that it's not until the whole thing's finished that you can see how it will work. If, like Lange, you always know where you're ultimately going, this is a fascinating method of working, almost like stripping down a car engine and replacing any dubious components with the best you can get until you've turned a Ford Cortina into a Ferrari – it's still a car, but an enormous improvement. Of course, Lange has his critics, those who believe that by disrupting the original spark, he is doing precisely the opposite. There are many who prefer their rock'n'roll to have a rough edge, to include mistakes, to breathe spontaneity. Certainly Def Leppard do stand accused of having too much polish when a little spit might have served them better, or at least been more interesting. On the other hand, nine million sales of *Pyromania* suggest that plenty of people would back the band and the producer in their quest for perfection.

With Lange now so clearly out of the equation, Def Leppard were left in a corner, the more so since studio time was already booked. Casting around for possible alternatives to Lange, many names were suggested, including Phil Collins. With a solo album – *No Jacket Required* – nearing completion, he was available but, as he had a world tour of his own to start in February 1985, Leppard felt they would be compromised by having to complete an album in such a relatively short space of time. That was a shame in many ways, for

Collins' instinctive grasp of radio friendly pop would have worked well alongside Leppard's songs, while his belief in not losing the initial spirit of a song would have been a striking contrast to *Pyromania* and all the more interesting for that. The complete opposite of Lange, Collins has such an attachment to the original writing sessions that he often uses his home demos as the basic backing track for a song, adding further instrumentation, proper drums and vocals, later in a full-scale recording facility. Working that way might have been a refreshing change for Leppard.

However, they remained committed to the large-scale production, arguing that the intimacy of Collins' method would be out of place in the arenas that they were playing and in the songs that they were writing. The search was still on for a suitable producer. It's been noted already that while in many respects, *Pyromania* updated Queen's work, taking it on into the 1980s, the most obvious reference point was Meat Loaf. Similarly over the top, featuring layer upon layer of studio trickery, vocals and effects, Meat Loaf's *Bat out of Hell* had been every bit as all-encompassing and sonically overwhelming as *Pyromania*. Much of the credit for that sound had to go to writer and producer Jim Steinman who, in the aftermath of that success, produced his own solo record, *Bad for Good*.

With its melodramatic flavour and epic operatic construction, that album had indicated that Steinman was very definitely the power behind the ample throne, his work with the likes of Bonnie Tyler on 'Total eclipse of the heart' merely underscoring the fact. As Joe pointed out, 'Jim Steinman was genuinely interested and seemed to have the credentials at the time, someone who was musical and technical.' He seemed the obvious candidate and so the band moved into Wisseloord Studios, Hilversum to begin work with him.

The sessions were shambolic, Steinman imposing his method of working on the band, while simultaneously attempting to impose his vision on them too. If Mutt Lange had had very clear and defined ideas as to what Leppard should sound like, they were empathic with the band's own goals. Steinman's tastes and those of the group did not dovetail so happily and the result was regular conflict between the two parties. There was no meeting of minds. Steinman later accused the band of lacking intelligence and of being incapable of playing songs together in the studio, feeling that they should record 'live', allowing him to overdub later. For their part, Leppard found Steinman dictatorial and completely at sea when working on material that he had not had a hand in writing and were alarmed by his refusal to allow them to follow the step-by-step recording practices they'd evolved with Lange. In a nutshell, 'after a couple of months, we realized we were just making a substandard version of *Pyromania*' according to Elliott. 'It was a Meat Loaf album, totally reliant on the sound through masses and masses of overdubs in the orchestral sense rather than in the tight sense which we were used to doing. We listened to what we'd done, didn't like any of it and scrapped the lot.'

By November, Steinman was sacked and all the work done so far consigned to the bin at huge cost. That reflects well on Def Leppard's drive to make an album they could stand behind, for if they were solely motivated by money, they could have rushed the Steinman product out for February 1985 and still sold in the region of five or six million off the back of *Pyromania*. However, it does call into question their attitude to the studio, for though Steinman obviously was not the right man for the job, their intransigence betrayed both inflexibility and a lack of confidence. Mutt Lange himself had tried to instil the belief into the band that they did not need him around any longer, that indeed, with a good engineer on board, they should have learned enough to produce themselves. They had spent a full year in the studio with Lange after all, plenty of time to pick up the tricks of the trade. It was clear that the band did not share those views, hence the engagement of Steinman. Yet once they had him, they apparently expected him to work in precisely the same way that Lange had, an impossibility, for no two producers – certainly no two such successful and highly individualistic producers – have the same methodology. If you call in a new producer, it should be because you want to stretch out, experiment and look for a different approach as had been the case when they changed from Allom to Lange for *High'n'Dry*. Leppard's whole approach to the Steinman sessions betrayed a lack of adventurousness that belied their avowed desire to break new ground again.

Stuck in Holland, the band went back to Mutt's advice and, bringing in Nigel Green, Lange's engineer, chose to produce the album themselves. In the few weeks that remained before the Christmas break, they set to work with a vengeance, Savage taking on the mantle of responsibility, overseeing the production and cracking the whip accordingly. Freed of what they felt had been Steinman's disruptive presence, the atmosphere improved almost at once and Joe felt that 'once we brought in Nigel and got down to it, we heard a massive improvement right away'. Although they'd not really got going as yet, merely laying the ground rules and rehearsing some material, they split up for Christmas with renewed optimism, looking forward to resuming work in earnest on 3 January 1985.

It's an old tradition to look forward to a new year, as though a mere change in the calendar will somehow magically usher in a brand new world where all your problems can be put behind you. Def Leppard's new year saw their problems only just beginning, for they were hit by tragedy. Driving to his parents' home in Sheffield along with Dutch girlfriend Miriam Barendsen in his distinctive and very powerful Corvette Stingray, Rick Allen and the driver of an Alfa Romeo became involved in a fairly juvenile argument, the other driver surging past and then holding Allen up. In a moment of madness, Allen tried to overtake, not seeing a left hand bend in the road since the Stingray was a left-hand drive vehicle. The Corvette clipped a wall on the bend, flew out of control and rolled over. The impact was shattering, with Rick hurled through the windscreen with such force that his left arm was sheared off by the restraining seatbelt. Miriam was, fortunately, less seriously injured, receiving some heavy bruising.

Miraculously, the first person on the scene was a local nurse, the second, another nurse who was driving by. They were able to calm the still-conscious Allen and, packing the severed arm in ice, they arranged for him to be rushed to the Royal Hallamshire Hospital in Sheffield where microsurgeons operated almost immediately. In a protracted operation, the arm was reattached. By now, news of Rick's accident was starting to reach the rest of the group and each spent a traumatic and dismal New Year's Eve lost in their own thoughts, hoping that Rick would pull through, for though his arm was clearly the main source of concern, he was on the critical list. All worries about making records went out of the window as they feared for their friend's life. Joe made it clear where their priorities lay, pointing out that 'when something like that happens, music becomes as important as Kleenex toilet rolls. It's nothing, a job, an industry, like making nuts and bolts. When you put it in perspective, it's fuck all. Here was a guy who might die. It was awful, he was on that critical list for 48 hours'.

Though the arm had been successfully sewn back and was thankfully free from any further injury, over the course of the next couple of days, it became clear that the operation had not succeeded. The damage inflicted on the tissue had been far too extensive for the arm to function again. An infection set in and the medical staff were left with no alternative but to amputate. Allen was kept under sedation and later revealed 'I was never aware that they tried to put the arm back on and I'm glad I didn't find out until later on.' When his medication was reduced and he regained normal consciousness, he was devastated by his 'disabled' state, understandably gaining little consolation from the news that his life was no longer in danger and that he would make a full recovery. What kind of a recovery would it be, what kind of life would it be if he had to quit the band, the band that had been his life for seven years? 'I had my usual pile of tapes with me and I'd hear the drums and think "I used to do that".'

It's scarcely credible, for even Hollywood would have to think twice before daring to produce a script so corny, but it was Def Leppard that pulled Allen through. As he told *Sounds* 'if I hadn't been in Def Leppard then I would have been out on a limb, 'scuse the pun! The rest of the boys were my lifeline. If I'd been doing any other kind of job . . . this is the only thing I've ever been able to do. I'm not too bright, I can't really count . . . playing the drums since I was ten years old has pretty much been my life'. Even so, in the days immediately following the crash, playing drums again was an aspiration rather than merely a matter of time. The chances of actually being able to play in a professional rock band such as Def Leppard, a band that prided itself on the precision of its sound, seemed little more than a pipe dream. Bands with one-armed drummers were few and far between – the absolute minimum requirement for a drummer is usually a full complement of arms and legs, so the future was indeed bleak.

Over the years, Allen has been lauded as a beacon of heroism in a dark and cowardly world. His courage and determination are not in doubt and will be dealt with later, but at the same time, let's get things into perspective. Although it looked very much as though his livelihood had gone, materially, he remained in an enviable position. He was one-fifth of a group with more than ten million album sales to its name, after all. If it came to the point where he could not work again, although that would be a grievous blow to his self-esteem and would rob him of his greatest passion, it would not leave him destitute. Month after month, we read in the papers of someone who has suffered similarly horrendous injuries and is then consigned to a life at the margins of society, eking out an existence on meagre invalidity benefits, while confined to their homes. On the same point, Rick and the Leppard organization had the financial wherewithal to enable him to rehabilitate properly after the crash. He would be able to have the use of the best medical and psychological care that money could buy, the opportunity to retrain and learn other skills and the certainty of a place within Leppard's operations should he want it. In that sense, the fearful blow was somewhat cushioned.

All his advantages were of little consolation to Rick at a time when he could only think that his career had come to a close. His friends in the band were equally distraught, Elliott remembering that he wept until his eyes were drained, Savage recalling an evening spent in stunned silence, Clark and Collen wrapping themselves around a bottle or two in their Parisian apartments. Savage and Elliott visited Allen and were amazed to find him in relatively good heart, surrounded by letters and gifts from well-wishers. Rick ultimately received around half a million letters from all over the globe and these helped his spirits when he was left in the hospital while the band returned to Holland, though of course they all continued to pay flying visits to him.

Sessions in Hilversum were, inevitably, sombre. Fortunately, Allen had completed most of the backing tracks before Christmas, so there was plenty to get on with but, though they tried to throw themselves into their work as a means of taking their mind off his plight, things moved slowly. As January wore on, better news began to filter through. Accompanied by his pile of cassettes, Rick had begun banging his feet against the bottom of his bed, tapping out the rhythms of these favourite songs. He started to wonder whether or not this might offer him a way of coping with his loss – could his feet do what his left arm had been accustomed to doing? It all seemed a little far fetched until he received a visit from Mutt Lange and began to talk to him about the possibilities. Lange was immediately enthusiastic and started to list all the available technology that might help Allen to play again. Once Lange had finished, Rick had a real goal to aim for – if the master of the studio environment saw no problems, why should he worry?

The rest of the band were delighted to hear that Rick was no longer in the doldrums and was beginning to battle his way back to fitness. Later on, they were all clear that the decision to continue or not had always been left to Allen, that they would wait until he was ready, but they would not have been human if they hadn't begun to think about replacements. Joe later posed the question 'would you kick your brother out if he lost his arm?', though that did beg the question 'would you kick your brother out if he had a drink problem' as Pete Willis had had. Nevertheless, their commitment to Rick was highly laudable and once he made the decision to work his way back into the band, they were completely behind him. Joe explained 'there was no mass depression, no "I can't do it man". We gave him encouragement, we took the piss out of him. Phil and Steve went to see him in hospital and they were calling him an inconsiderate bastard. And it worked! He knew we were rooting for him'.

Behind the playful jibes was real concern of course, for these extensive delays were further harming the band's future. It does speak volumes that the other members of the band, the management and the company stayed behind Allen – though had they chosen to do otherwise they would have been crucified in the media – but it cannot have been an easy decision as the months were slipping away and new *Pyromania* inspired imitators were taking to the airwaves.

It's ludicrous to call Allen 'lucky' when such terrible injuries had been inflicted upon him but, if it was going to happen, it happened at the least inopportune time. He was fortunate perhaps that the Steinman sessions had been aborted and that the album was being started again from scratch. Had it been on the brink of completion with a world tour ready to go, would they have been able to wait for him? Booking venues is an expensive business and failing to play costs a lot of money. If the new album had been ready to hit the racks, Allen's position might have looked a little more tenuous – at the very least, they would almost certainly have had to tour with a replacement, leaving Rick with a couple of years in which to kick his heels. And if the session drummer fitted in well, who knows what the future might have held.

In the same way, developments in recorded sound meant that returning to the band would be far easier than a handful of years before. With the increasing prevalence of electronic drums – ideal for the sounds Leppard wanted – and the introduction of sophisticated sampling keyboards such as the Fairlight, it would now be perfectly possible for Rick to program a vast range of drum sounds and play them through a computer. Once more, Leppard's financial security ensured that whatever instrument was needed, Rick could have it, a luxury not extended to bands lower down the scale. Had only acoustic drums been available, it would have been much harder for him to become sufficiently proficient in the space of time he had. Rick accepted that, saying 'I never thought about still using an acoustic drum kit for a second. We worked out a combination of electronic pads which I play with my right hand and foot pedals which play pretty much what I did with the left.'

Acoustic drums were all that was available as the band were forming and making their earliest recordings. If Allen had lost his arm back in 1980, the technology would not have been there for him. Not only that, but since Leppard were far from being an established act, the luxury of time would not have been there either. Even now, they needed to get on with making the record as quickly as possible but, with the success of *Pyromania* behind them, such delays were inconvenient rather than career threatening. Once more, it's hard to see how Allen could have retained his seat at the drums if the accident had happened during the recording of *On through the night*. Perhaps the band would have been strong enough to wait for him but the record company would not. For all their protestations that Allen is like a brother, Leppard are hard-headed enough when it comes to business not to take any prisoners. Maybe Willis' problems were more self-inflicted, perhaps it was harder to feel sympathy for an obnoxious drinker than a mate lying in a hospital bed with horrific injuries, but if Allen's injuries had threatened to sabotage their career, surely he would have been eased out, at least temporarily.

But let none of that obscure the fact that the band were compassionate in the extreme in allowing Rick the chance to return to the fold when he was, nor the importance of their encouragement in helping him overcome the enormous obstacles that were in his way. Above all, do not dismiss the enormous reserves of courage, dedication and determination that Allen possesses, upon which he drew so extensively and which allowed him to regain his place in the vanguard of rock drummers. Not only did he overcome a physical disability which would have beaten many, he had the mental strength alongside the natural talent to learn a whole new way of playing his instrument, a monumental task given that he'd been playing drums for a decade or more. Now he had to forget all he knew, all that was instinctive and start all over again. Rick was a shining example to the rest of the band who were getting themselves bogged down with the new record, giving it neither the concentration nor the enthusiasm it required. Allen's efforts spurred them on, forcing them to keep up the pace so that they wouldn't be letting him down. It was a task that proved largely beyond them, for Joe was forced to confess that 'we tried to put a brave face on it but we just fell apart. Nothing got done, literally, until Rick came back'.

The band were unstinting in their praise for Rick and for the part he played in keeping their spirits up in the darkest hours. Joe admitted that 'he's the most strong minded person I know. In hospital he was banging his feet and once he'd decided he could transfer what he did with his left arm to his left leg, he had a guy design a kit for him and disappeared. He got himself locked away in a room 'cos he didn't want anybody to hear him re-learning and then one day, four months later he came back and he was playing again. He said "come and hear this" and he played "When the levee breaks" and it sounded brilliant, tear-jerking time.'

Rick's return was unquestionably the high point of the whole long, drawn out recording process. Now that he was back, the band could have been forgiven for thinking that after losing two producers and almost losing a friend, no more traumas could possibly beset them. Wrong. Rick coming back to play with the band was a fillip, but he found a record that was in a state of disarray. Though things had gone better with Nigel Green, they were still far from the perfection for which they strived. Mutt Lange had kept a watching brief through it all, listening to recordings, offering advice, tinkering here and there. By April when the five piece were reunited, it was obvious that another kind of major surgery would be necessary – on the album. They worked on it further, and in July Lange was given all they'd done to date.

He was frank in his assessment, informing them that they were making the same record they'd made the last time, that the song structures needed a lot of work, that some of the material had to be rewritten and some of the songs were beyond redemption. With this damning verdict ringing in their ears, a verdict with which they broadly concurred, the band decided that once again, they'd wait for Mutt to help them put things right. Having spent very nearly a year on the album, everything they had was consigned to the dustbin – two and a half years on from *Pyromania*, a new record was not on the horizon.

Their reliance on Lange enabled dissident voices to claim that Leppard were little more than a manufactured band, a band that were all at sea without Lange's guiding influence, a band of no native ability. These barbed comments were harsh, but forgivable given the shocking state they were in. Eighteen months since their previous tour had finished and they still hadn't recorded a note of new music. It didn't bode well for the future, nor did it improve their reputation. But that was to ignore the traumatic times they'd gone through. Steinman had been a mistake, plain and simple and surely everybody is allowed a mistake. They'd recognized their error and acted quickly to correct it. That was bold and showed great strength of purpose, but it must have dented their confidence when a successful producer like Steinman used his time in the studio to berate them.

Even then, things could have been salvaged. Working with Green and producing themselves was another enterprising strategy which might well have worked. Just as things were starting to move, the band were turned upside down by Allen's accident. Steve Clark's own drink problem was also cause for concern, and ultimately his contribution to the album was a comparatively small one. Hit for six, it was hardly a surprise to find that they were not fully focused while in the studio. Since their work was built around a compulsive attention to detail, a lack of concentration was a fatal flaw, hence the problems with the material that Lange identified.

Though these are reasons rather than excuses, they cannot fully cover Leppard's sudden decline from kings of the studio to shambling novices. A lot of the blame must be put on the pressure they were under. Following up a multi-million seller is a demanding business, for suddenly you're put in a very new and different position. Putting together *Pyromania*, Def Leppard were just another band on the Phonogram roster hoping to piece together a good record and looking to make the breakthrough. With nothing to lose, they were able to play with greater freedom. Now, as one of the top handful of acts in the world, everything had changed. The eyes of the world were on them, wondering if they could do it again. They themselves had the pressure of producing a record that was better than the predecessor; no easy task. Financial pressures were immense too, not necessarily on a personal level but because so many people now depended upon them as a source of income – the people in the management office, at Phonogram, promoters, road crew and many others were reliant upon Def Leppard coming up with the goods again, for Leppard's success paid their wages. As a consequence, Leppard were putting together a carbon copy of *Pyromania*, for they didn't have the nerve to do anything else. That was the nub, a failure of nerve rather than of ability.

Man management in the studio is as much a part of the producer's job as any technical expertise – it was one of the reasons for Steinman's failure just as it was a fundamental part of Lange's success. Lange understood the band and knew how to guide them to get the very best out of them. Once he was back on board, although things were never going to progress quickly – that simply wasn't his style – they did progress effectively. According to Joe 'Mutt came back in July 1985 but we had to leave Holland, because our time there had run out. The two of us went to Paris to do vocals for the backing tracks but after a month we had to get out because there was no air conditioning and he had to go out every twenty minutes because he was collapsing.' Unable to acclimatize to the Studio Des Dames, Leppard booked in to the Windmill Lane facility in Dublin, home to U2.

Slowly but surely, the project began to take on its own life as they fell back into the routines that had served them so well on *Pyromania*. Even so, after a period of almost a year where at least one member of the band was always working in the studio, they began to get itchy feet. They'd already done some rehearsals in the summer of 1985 for a tour that had to be aborted owing to their recording difficulties. With the following summer fast approaching, an invitation was extended to them to play the 'Monsters of Rock' festivals across Europe. The chance to blow away the cobwebs was an absolute Godsend for them, giving a chance to escape from the rigours of Lange's working patterns for a few weeks. It would also provide them with an opportunity to assess Rick's state of health and his ability to play a live show, a very different discipline to that of playing in the studio. If he could cope with these gigs, the chances were that he would be able to handle the extensive touring that would accompany the new record's release. If it became too much for him, contingency plans would be necessary.

To offer a safety net, Status Quo's drummer Jeff Rich was recruited for these few shows so that Rick would not be so exposed. The first show was played in Cork's Connolly Hall in August 1986, *Hot Press*' Tony O'Donoghue writing that 'Rick Allen gave a stunning performance of courage, passion and skill. A most exceptional example of resilience and fortitude'. O'Donoghue was ironically, confirming one of the group's greatest fears as Joe explained: 'I hope we don't get the sympathy vote. The last thing I'd want is for the album to get five stars out of kindness, out of fair play to us for keeping Rick on. I'd get really annoyed.' Such approbation could not be avoided though, for it even helped the British warm to them at long last.

The only British show would be at Donington, where Leppard would be third on Ozzy Osbourne's bill. Prior to that though, further warm-ups were planned in Ireland. Rich had other commitments with Status Quo in mainland Europe but had agreed to fly back in time for Leppard's show in Ballybunion. He missed his flight in Stockholm and then the taxi bringing him on the hour and a half journey from Dublin to the gig broke down in the middle of nowhere. Meanwhile, in the midst of rural Ireland, Rick Allen was getting increasingly nervous as show time approached. The die was cast – Rick had to play alone for the first time. The fairytale return was complete, with Jeff Rich turning up in time to see that he was now redundant and could return to Status Quo.

Donington was next on the agenda and Leppard were lucky to survive it for Phonogram had got things horribly wrong again. The week of the festival, the music papers carried a full page advert for Leppard saying 'They're back. Simply the greatest rock band in the world'. Perhaps it was meant to be ironic after the prolonged hiatus but given Britain's jaundiced attitude towards the band, it was not very clever. Ultimately, though the band were decidedly rusty and lacklustre, the show was salvaged by a crowd that were actually willing them to succeed, happy to forgive past misdemeanours out of respect and admiration for the way they'd fought back in the face of adversity. Rick received an astonishing response that simply overwhelmed him and by the end of the show, it was obvious that if their fourth album was anything like, they had a ready-made audience that were gagging for it.

One major show was left, at the 'Monsters' festival in Mannheim. The European arm of Phonogram turned out in numbers to see if they still had a band worth promoting. In pouring rain, soaked to the skin and with possibly the worst live sound they'd ever had, Leppard trudged through their set, indignity heaped upon indignity. To the company people, it was enough just to see the band back on stage, but for the band it was yet another disaster in a thoroughly exasperating year. Showing a nice line in self-deprecating humour, the band included a photo from the gig in the booklet that went with the new album on its eventual release. The caption read 'Life at the top 84-87'.

For it would be 1987 before the album saw the light of day. Heading back to Holland to complete work after the shows were over, Joe immediately contracted a serious bout of mumps which left him in quarantine for a couple of weeks and put the band even further behind schedule. As Joe returned, Mutt was involved in a car crash on his way into the studio. He was fortunate to escape with leg injuries that allowed him to be back at work within three weeks, but these constant traumas were just wearing the band down. If they'd been Led Zeppelin, talk would have been of Faustian pacts. Leppard, though, were too normal for that kind of nonsense for as Peter Mensch ruefully pointed out 'Def Leppard will never be famous like Led Zeppelin in that way because they're just not controversial. It's all down to the material and the show'. All they could do was brace themselves for further months in the studio, reconcile themselves to another missed release date – January 1987 this time – and hope that by the following Christmas, they might have finally completed work on an album that was turning into a nightmare.

The album finally had a name too, *Hysteria*, as Joe explained. 'It was Rick's idea, after all the stuff that went on with his accident. It got pretty close to hysteria two days after the accident – reception area of the hospital was teeming with newspaper reporters and kids and because we weren't all that popular in England at the time, it made it appear more massive. Rick was on the front of the *Daily Star* and it was like he was the Queen or Ian Botham or something. We had to be snuck in through the fuckin' laundry chute to go see him.' The title was a late decision for as Joe recalled 'it was going to be called "Animal Instincts" but then we thought that sounded really stupid. We had the sleeve ready, so that was another four grand down the drain. But it just wasn't right.'

Their absence from the scene had thrown another potential problem into the melting pot. With *Pyromania* having broken the mould, it was inevitable that others would follow their lead. In their enforced absence, Leppard had seen countless other groups aping their sound, some intelligently, others blatantly copying what they saw as the formula. In the light of all that, the band stiffened their resolve to produce something that would again leave the competition standing, hence the additional studio time required. Most notable of all was the release in the autumn of 1986 of Bon Jovi's third record *Slippery when wet*. Crammed with hit singles, the album had elevated Bon Jovi to the top of the heap after they had released two poorly received records. Jon had replaced Joe as the number one sex symbol in the rock music field and had usurped much of the audience too. It was a worrying development in some ways, for where *Pyromania* had given people something they couldn't get elsewhere, now there was no shortage of similar albums. Elliott shrugged off the problem. 'We couldn't really take what we had with *Pyromania* any further. So many people have improved on our sound over the past few years when we didn't have the chance to that there was no point in doing the same thing. It's fair to say that we did create something new within a very old-fashioned form of music with *Pyromania*. And a lot of people copied it. I take it as a compliment! Now there's Bon Jovi, Poison, Whitesnake, Cinderella – if this album can sell four million in that sort of company, then it'll have done well. But I'd rather have an album do well in that market than if there were no other rock albums about.'

Having to rethink their whole style was easier said than done. As Lange had observed, some of their earlier songs were '*Pyromania* by numbers' and it took a fundamental rethink to come up with something new once more. Pioneering is never easy and at times Joe's temper snapped when having to justify his existence. 'Look, if we had never existed, Bon Jovi would probably have never existed. What they're doing is what we were doing three years ago. Good luck to them – I think they'd say we were their favourite band. I think they're really good . . . They've just kept our seat warm for the past two years and it's time for them to move over. Bye bye lads!' Not one of his better predictions, for there was more than enough room for both groups to coexist perfectly happily. By August 1987 when the new album finally emerged, much of Bon Jovi's initial impetus had started to run out and the world was ready for Leppard to take over from them for a while.

Eventually, at an estimated cost of £1 million and after three years of solid work, *Hysteria* was in the shops. Now, no record can justify that kind of outlay or that amount of time and it's stupid to try, so the band and Phonogram simply decided to let the music do the talking for them, Joe trying to deflate things by merely noting that 'after spending so much time on this, if there's anything wrong with it then we need a jolly good kick up the bottom. If we've got it wrong . . . well, we could have got it wrong in three weeks'.

Hysteria didn't so much talk as bawl at the top of its voice for it was nothing if not a very good, state of the art, technological rock record. While U2 were simplifying down to folk song structures, Leppard were involved in a 'kitchen sink' production, invoking huge walls of sound in the way that Phil Spector had twenty years previously. Though there were attempts to suggest that this album was radically different to its predecessor, such claims were rubbish. With the charts teeming with the likes of Bon Jovi, Ratt, Motley Crue and Whitesnake, it was readily apparent that metal lite still held sway in the public mind. With an investment of £1 million to recoup, taking chances was neither sensible nor practical. In *Hysteria*, Leppard provided the fans with a record very much rooted in *Pyromania* but showing a degree of progression. Its strengths were consolidated while its weaknesses – the rambling nature of some songs, the tendency to overplay – had been remedied. In essence, it was Leppard reminding all and sundry that there might be plenty of imitators, but the originals were still the best, though in fairness, Bon Jovi did have legitimate claims to their crown.

Improving on *Pyromania* was a tough task, but they were up to it despite the distractions. Rick Savage was quick to point out that 'we always wanted to keep songs concise and not self-indulgent. People think we've changed our style to get a wider audience but we haven't. We've just improved in the way we always wanted to.' Certainly, Leppard were more radio friendly than they'd ever been before, but whether that was natural progression or merely a product of the need to sell records has to be a matter of opinion. One contributory factor was the change in Allen's drumming style. Always a skilled player, his style had been rather busy, showing the audience how good he was, sometimes to the detriment of the song. Now, presumably because of circumstances, he was less obtrusive and his drumming was almost skeletal at times. In turn, songs tended to be simpler and if there's one recipe for rock radio success, it's keep it big and dumb, the bigger and dumber the better. What better example of that could there be than 'Pour some sugar on me', a single which reached number two in the States. Almost a terrace anthem a la 'We are the champions', its choruses, carefully crafted, were built round a hook that led inexorably to a huge black hole that simply sucked in the unwary listener. Kiss without the make-up, Slade without the top hat, Mott by any other name, it was classic glam boasting a guitar riff you could play in your sleep.

Joe was largely responsible for the song which he described as 'just Gary Glitter meets the Sweet but still sounding like us. We've always been a rock band, not a heavy metal band'. Its potential as a single was absolutely crucial to the prospects of *Hysteria* as a whole. Joe understood the machinations of the market place pretty well by now and accepted the need for hits. They had worked hard to produce them and he was happy with the results:

'I seriously believe that we've got up to five hit singles on this record, even "Rocket", though it's such an unusual song and such a change from something like "Pour some sugar on me", which is an obvious shot at the commercial market. The chorus is three chords – I wrote it like that 'cos it's all I can play, I always have to think commercially. I can't write "Gods of war". When I pick up a guitar, I tend to play "Wild thing" a lot better than "All along the watchtower". Peter Mensch is totally right. You cannot survive without hit singles these days because AOR radio in America isn't responsible for breaking bands any more. *Slippery when wet* sold eight million copies through the singles. There was a period where people were really snobby about hits, that it wasn't credible. That's the most ridiculous thing. I like being on *Top of the Pops*, I find it funny. Ninety-eight per cent of our stuff is tongue-in-cheek anyway. When you've got a rhinoceros in one of your videos, you can't take yourselves that seriously.'

Elliott was right that AOR radio was no longer so important. MTV had taken over that responsibility now, something Leppard had benefited from already when the clip for 'Photograph' had launched *Pyromania*. Bearing that in mind, prior to releasing *Hysteria*, they seemed to have stopped off for a visit to the stylists – the carefully distressed jeans and jackets of 1987 were a marked contrast to the rough and ready Union Jack raggedness of four years earlier – so they would be made even more welcome on MTV. To make the most of this TV exposure, songs had to be further simplified, purely because the sound quality on television did not really compare with radio, since stereo broadcasting was still in its infancy. All the extraneous sound had to be cut away for a song to cut through. For that reason, *Hysteria* was perhaps not so aggressive as *Pyromania*, but more polished. They'd added a danceable quality to the tunes too which did them no harm at all given that on MTV their songs rubbed up alongside the likes of Madonna and the Jackson clan.

One of the more inventive tracks on the record, one of its best, was 'Rocket', which in parts was reminiscent of Malcolm McLaren's 'Buffalo gals', not a comparison that would have sprung readily to mind in the past! The use of sound effects was beginning to sound a little jaded now but the rhythmic opening was genuinely enthralling. Sounding like something from the drummers of Burundi, a sound that artists as diverse as Echo and the Bunnymen, Peter Gabriel, Adam Ant and Bow Wow Wow had employed to good effect, it had never been used in a rock setting before. It was a very adventurous move that opened them up to criticism from the traditionalists but one which showed that creative atrophy had yet to set in. 'Rocket' was clean and pristine, light, poppy and a genuine rush of singalong fun, a virtual rap name-checking the band's heroes such as Bowie, Beatles, Elton John, Queen and Thin Lizzy before ending in a wild rhythmic section.

Equally interesting was Steve Clark's 'Gods of war'. Musically in similar territory to 'Switch 625' at times, the brooding introduction and spellbinding guitar figure made it clear that here was a more mature work, dark and intense. The anti-war, 'why are we fighting?' statement was scarcely new, but it's a sentiment that bears repetition. The song marked Clark's emergence as a major writer and offered such promise for the future, promise that would never be fulfilled.

On the other side of the coin, 'Animal' was an equally assured piece of work, brilliant pop music which was to be accompanied by a daft video, an unbeatable combination as promos such as Gabriel's 'Sledgehammer' or New Order's 'True faith' have proved. The crystal clear clarion guitar – that year's sound, Guns N'Roses' 'Sweet child o'mine' working on the same principle – heralded a lovely, simple melody, affecting, throaty vocals and an engaging drum pattern.

Obvious crowd-pleasing, hands in the air fare, the final call of 'Animal' was blatant audience participation/manipulation stuff, perfect for singalongs in the company of 15,000 people. There were few better rock singles that year.

It was however in what was now termed Bon Jovi territory, which tended to irritate more than somewhat. Joe had resigned himself to his fate. 'I can see it now. "Def Leppard – the new Bon Jovi". And it's just because we're a rock band. There's been Bon Jovi, there's been Europe and hopefully there'll be Def Leppard. But we can't be *just* Def Leppard because we're a rock band and people are prejudiced against rock bands.' It was richly ironic that Def Leppard, a band from Sheffield, had paved the way for Bon Jovi's success back in America. Repaying the favour, it was Bon Jovi's single success that finally awakened the British pop audience to Leppard's charms. With New Jersey's finest having totted up three top twenty singles in the UK – 'You give love a bad name', 'Livin' on a prayer' and 'Wanted dead or alive' – fans were ready for more in that style. 'Animal' provided it, racing to number six in the charts, comfortably their best performance to date at home. Lyrically of course, it remained undemanding, but Joe tried to defend his words, arguing that it made a point about basic instincts: 'Men can't help it, it's in our genes. All this sexist crap that's thrown at us annoys me because no matter how educated we get, we're still animals and sometimes the primal takes over.'

The single buyers rushed out to pick up *Hysteria*, finding much to enjoy and giving the band their first British number one album into the bargain. 'Love bites', which gave them a number one in the States showcased a band that was continuing to mature with a deeper lyric ruminating on love and betrayal, building gradually to a powerful crescendo. Classic epic pop in the 10CC style, it made it obvious that Leppard were not willing to be pigeonholed as hairy old rockers, but had other talents on which to build. As songwriters, they certainly had improved. *Hysteria* itself was a case in point, a reflective ballad that was a nice change in pace. Halting and hesitant, it indicated a group that was still struggling to come to terms with the form, but one that was striving in the right direction, not content to allocate time to plodding filler rock but willing to stretch themselves further.

'Run Riot' was a leftover of sorts, Leppard doing what they'd done best in the past. AC/DC-influenced following a beautifully distorted guitar introduction, the sheer tempo of the song allowed them to concoct a genuinely thrilling rush of excitement. Its constituent parts all seemed hopelessly slight yet the final combination was compelling, evidence of Lange's invaluable handiwork, underlining his priceless value to the group. 'Don't shoot shotgun' shared similar characteristics, with Allen's imagination working overtime as he searched for inventive new rhythm patterns, his new restraint leaving holes for the vocals to fill, while the seductive backing vocals were once again employed effectively. 'A leaf out of Queen's book I'm afraid' Elliott was forced to admit. 'I don't do them, it's Mutt, Phil and Sav so we get a different blend.' The backing vocals on the title track reputedly featured 200 voices!

Although the album project had been a harrowing, frustrating and exhausting process, there was still room for some daftness, highlighting the way in which the professional band could separate themselves from the private traumas when they were at work. 'Women', the obligatory raucous opener was tight, taut and crass; 'Armageddon it' was packed with thoroughly dumb double entendre, though again, love it or loathe it, it provided a compulsive singalong chorus; 'Excitable' was the 'Rock of ages' style joker in the pack, the hyped up heavy breathing and clanging guitar proving that it should be taken with a pinch of salt. Like much of *Hysteria*, it all relied a little too heavily on stomping choruses that were all too familiar in the days of the Gary Glitter shouts, but they were hugely likeable and played with a knowing irony that deflected any latent pomposity.

The final song, 'Love and affection', was probably the most atypical track on the album, a huge power ballad, a love song that set the protagonists against the world. Very corny 'you and me babe' stuff, as the track played out you could visualize a huge mirrorball reflecting across the dancefloor, and yet it still managed to be emotionally affecting. Though it wasn't standard Leppard fare musically, the atmosphere of the song was very revealing and said a great deal about just why it was that Def Leppard were so successful.

Def Leppard's music is all about happy endings, no loose ends, about everything working out, about taking refuge in the arms of your partner. Leppard are melodramatic, they're corny at times but they're also heartwarming in the way that Hollywood's most popular movies are. You can participate in a Leppard song and come out the other end feeling better about yourself. It may be hopelessly superficial, but it is a tempting escape route from a world of increasing uncertainty. Def Leppard's *Hysteria* didn't make any demands on you and merely tried to make you feel good to be alive, promising to deliver a fun time if that was what you wanted. No-one gets hurt and we all live happily ever after, or at least for the sixty-minute duration of the album. If that sounds harsh, it's not meant to be for all music doesn't have to be angst-ridden or politically motivated. There's room for PJ Harvey just as there's room for Take That. You simply choose what suits you best and ignore the rest.

It must be said however that a quick run through Leppard's lyrics would leave you totally unaware of the tumultuous events that had wreaked such havoc in the preceding three years. In a live review, *Melody Maker*'s Carol Clerk wrote that 'unashamedly escapist, Def Leppard are the first to admit that "there isn't any major intelligence in our lyrics and we don't put them on the sleeve because they don't read very well!"' But how could any serious artist have failed to channel such personal tragedies into their work? It is impossible. The only conclusion was that Def Leppard might be deadly serious about their work but they were not serious artists in the Neil Young sense of the phrase. Elliott held up his hands to the charge but was unconcerned by it. 'Some people seem to forget that everything you do doesn't have to have some kind of social statement. I have opinions, but I don't sing songs about it . . . a kid on the dole doesn't want to hear a record about being on the dole. I'd rather write "Pour some sugar on me", which totally makes no sense at all and the kid can make up his own mind about it. I'd sooner stick with the British approach which is totally ambiguous, doesn't say anything, doesn't mean anything, they just sound alright. *You* explain what T-Rex's lyrics are about. If you can figure his out, then you can figure mine out. "Hub-cap diamond star halo" means more to me than "I went down to the river" I'm afraid. To me, T-Rex make your imagination work harder. If I wrote from experience, I don't think it would sound very good, the last five-a-side game I had. I used to write that way, but it didn't work for us.' Each to his own, but it did seem a terrible waste of experience – just imagine what Elvis Costello would have made of all this emotional and physical carnage.

Whatever reservations there might have been, much of the press comment was favourable. In *Sounds*, Paul Elliott's five star review called it 'a progression of sorts, every bit as fresh and vital as back in '83 . . . Leppard's finest hour, [showing a] greater breadth and maturity . . . it will crack Britain wide open and make the band a household name in their backyard'. Prescient comment indeed, reinforced by *Hot Press*'s Jon De Leon. The paper's marking system termed it 'intoxicating', the review pointing out that 'it sets the standard for other metal-inclined rockers in 1987. It's hard to see it being surpassed'. It was left to *Q* to offer a dissenting voice, Emily Fraser arguing persuasively that 'a minority of us feel that the band have become sanitized by the experience and are now more polish than passion. There's little that makes a statement'.

One statement the band were keen to make was on the road where they saw themselves as an altogether superior proposition, Joe remarking with typical humility that 'even at our worst, we're 100 times better than anybody else'. They'd spent $100,000 on a conventional stage set when Peter Mensch was struck by the idea of playing in the round, the stage being set in the centre of the arena, the seating built around it. It was an audacious move, almost unique in rock music although Yes had dabbled with the concept back in 1978, the Police also trying it out in 1983. Mensch was thrilled with the idea, one which would mark Leppard out as being distinct from the Bon Jovis of the world. He explained the reasoning behind such an ambitious project: 'Well, A, it had never been done before by a hard rock band and B, it would give us more seats and every seat would be good. I figured that if you can play with a one-armed drummer, you can play in the round. It's like Edmund Hillary and Everest, you play it because it's there.' This would form the basis for the *Hysteria* tour, though inevitably certain venues weren't able to provide the necessary facilities and the band was forced to play conventional shows there, which is how they started promoting *Hysteria* in the UK.

Reviews were predictably mixed, *Melody Maker*'s Chris Roberts telling his readers more about himself than the band: 'Characterless and powerless. The singer is a repellent nouveau-riche navvy. They're not worth my time – I've been here a whole nine minutes when I see there's an exit fifteen yards away'. Paul Elliott was rather more enthusiastic in his review of the Nottingham gig: 'This wasn't perfect. Will great do?' Britain had finally been conquered as venues the length and breadth of the country sold out in double quick time. With the UK in the bag, it was time to resume their relationship with the States, in the round.

Never ones to shirk a challenge, the group threw themselves into the unknown with real vigour, creating problems for themselves in the process. Joe admitted that 'I'd be a liar if I said it wasn't exhausting. The first night we did it in the round, we'd done eight days' rehearsal but we still ended up trying to fill the stage too much and by the end of the first couple of songs everybody was looking for a bucket to throw up into. After three gigs though, we were really cookin'. We reached a certain fitness peak so that we can deal with it and the set's well paced enough to take care of itself. I enjoyed getting kinda hot and sweaty anyway.' Giving everyone in the auditorium a great sound and a great view, the set-up was ideal – MTV later adopted the idea, albeit on a smaller scale, for their 'Unplugged' series and for live specials by the likes of Bon Jovi. The spectacle was impressive and it did prevent fans concentrating solely on Rick Allen, something that had worried them. 'In the round' was a bigger innovation than a one-armed drummer as Joe agreed. 'There's nothing we can do short of playing upside down next time to top this. The novelty probably is taking a bit of weight off Rick but at the same time, when it features him, it features him more. He's not hidden behind the rest of us. I'd like to think that we'd play in the round on the next tour too, because playing at one end would be a bit of a downer now.'

The scale of the physical challenge required a whole new, professional attitude from the group. Phil Collen had already given up drinking after he'd bought a £6000 watch when so plastered he didn't know what he was doing. At the same time, Joe Elliott accepted he needed to have a radical rethink of his approach to his craft. The wilder days of yore, particularly in the company of the female fans, had to become a thing of the past as word of AIDS began to circulate. Alcohol had to come off the menu too for it did little for the voice. He explained that his overriding concern was the quality of the show.

> 'On the first tour, I went at it like a rat up a drainpipe but that's changed now. It gets to be really boring when you know it might be you tonight, someone from Ratt last night and somebody from Motley Crue tomorrow. I've got a steady girlfriend now. We used to do all that, but it would've been a bit weird if we hadn't. Five lads from Sheffield let loose in America? Come on! On the road, I don't drink or smoke, there's fewer parties. Now I can go on stage and perform better. The most important thing to me is those two hours a night and if the other twenty-two have to be really boring, then so be it. I'd rather go to a club until five in the morning 'cos I'm wide awake with all the adrenaline but I know I can't sing the night after if I do and for the sake of entertaining myself, I'm not gonna piss off 15,000 kids the following night by singing like Lemmy or somebody. That wouldn't suit the songs we do.'

It was an attitude that was beginning to permeate the whole business for, despite all of the wild stories that still did the rounds, the truth was that most musicians spent the evening 'in bed with their accounts and some sandwiches' as Bruce Dickinson once put it. The stakes were simply too high, too much money was hanging on the artists for them to have the luxury of getting wrecked and playing like idiots. Word soon gets round if a band plays a few bad gigs and acts with a total disregard for the fans, popularity can quickly take a nosedive. With recording and touring costs going through the roof, no-one could take that risk. If you're committed to a couple of years on the road, nothing must go wrong. Among the more seasoned pros, there was also a growing disenchantment with the stupidity of life on the road and the things that entertained them at nineteen bored them at twenty-seven. Joe for example had been mellowed by his time in Ireland. 'The people are very romantic, a lot more emotional than in England, it's nice there. If I'd spent eighteen months in Los Angeles, I'd be in a lunatic asylum. I can't handle the falseness, all that "hey man! Wanna party? I've got a bag of coke!" Fuck it! I'm not interested. I'd rather have a pint and talk about football.'

It's small wonder that bands on the road do go off the rails for it's a terribly tedious way of life, despite the seemingly glamorous trappings. During the first American leg of the *Hysteria* tour, Elliott accepted that 'the best part of being in a band is playing live. That's why we got together in the first place. We've always been a band who wanted to get it right on record, it's the only opportunity you have to try to create perfection. Live, you've got to entertain people. I don't really stand still and you can only really sing properly when you're stood still, but if I did, it'd look really silly. Half my job isn't singing, it's getting an audience going. We set such a standard on the records and what we do there, five people can't physically do, but we don't want to take out an orchestra, we want it to be us. That's where the fun comes in. But you have to do it in moderation to enjoy it. We were on the bus for six hours yesterday and you wouldn't believe how tiring that is day after day. Being on the road can weaken you, we've all gone down with something at some stage, you keep catching someone else's cold, it keeps doing the rounds. The food can be a problem. Phil and Rick are vegetarians, and when they ask for a vegetarian meal on the plane, they get fish. They live on peanuts most of the time! Hotels are really important to us. A good one has a mentholated steam room which is great for the voice, a gym and a good room service menu that's twenty-four hours a day. From there, backstage is our home. We've even set up studios wherever we can so that we can try to write on the road'.

Everything was focused on the gigs and rightly so. The concerts – a little gimmicky for some tastes, but undeniably strong both visually and musically – helped keep *Hysteria* in the public eye for more than a year. Finally, in July 1988, *Hysteria* became America's number one album after forty-nine weeks on the chart, spending the next few months fighting with Guns N'Roses' *Appetite for destruction* for the top spot. It was final compelling proof that everything they'd endured, all the work they'd put in to *Hysteria* had been worthwhile. Phil made it clear that 'we want to be successful, everyone does if they were honest enough to say it, but our popularity has come from a lot of hard work. We've all paid our dues in one way or another.' Joe felt it was vindication for their belief in the music before all else. 'If money meant that much to us, we wouldn't have spent so much making this album because we had to sell two million to get the costs back. That's the arrogant side of us. We thought we could sell five or six again, or even ten million.' When the returns were in, *Hysteria* had sold 14.2 million copies, a million of which came in the UK, *Melody Maker*'s Carol Clerk opining that 'Def Leppard are something vivid and friendly and intimate. They are something to get affectionate about, happy with, excited by'. Pleased to have made the grade back home, Joe still wasn't sure where his heart lay: 'At the moment I have a very love/hate relationship with England. I do miss my parents, but I don't miss the fact that you can't walk around at night without getting mugged. All the papers we have from England are full of stories about hooligans.' Three cheers for the tabloid press and their peerless ability to distort the facts.

With things going so well for them, Joe couldn't resist the opportunity to stir things up again, showing that all the youthful bravado had not petered out in his late-twenties. 'We're a pop band in the same way that Thin Lizzy were, they never lost their credibility with rock fans. I like the idea of a rock band crossing over and not having to totally wimp out. Okay, compared to Napalm Death, we're soft. All we've ever wanted to be is quite simply the biggest rock band in the world and you don't become that by sounding like Napalm Death. I'm not interested in getting great reviews and selling five records. I *like* playing the NEC and Wembley. I *like* standing on stage and seeing people out there. I think everybody's ambition is to sell as many records as you can and to play in front of as many people as you can. Even those fuckin' poxy little bands who say that's not their thing – they're lying.' Contradicting himself, he went on to add 'I don't believe it should all be based on sales. It should be judged on the sound of the bloody thing . . . we weren't afraid of losing what we'd gained with *Pyromania* because we didn't want to rush something out just to cash in on the success.'

Retaining the chip on his shoulder, smarting at the snobbery prevalent in the industry, even a BRIT Award nomination couldn't mollify him. 'It's nice to be nominated but we're never going to win anything. We're stuck in the mud heavy metal band – long hair and jeans. We can't vote for them can we? I like the fact that we're unfashionable – the black sheep in the charts, the black sheep on *Top of the Pops*, the black sheep in *Smash Hits* just because we're a rock band with two guitarists where everyone else has got capped teeth and happy haircuts. We have nothing in common with the Pet Shop Boys like we have nothing in common with Des O'Connor.'

Despite these irritations, they returned to Britain in spring 1988, able to play Wembley and the NEC, in the round, giving British fans the chance to see the full American production, a courtesy that not all groups extended to their supporters. *Sounds* reviewed the show, noting that 'they're boisterous and agile and openly thrilled to be home, hyper-ventilating with confidence. Britain has every reason to be proud of them'. Basking in such unusual hyperbole, Leppard were a tired, but delighted band, but one which took nothing for granted. Joe cast his mind back to shows much earlier in their career: 'We once did a gig at New Brighton Pavilion near Liverpool and eleven kids turned up and one of them was doing his homework. Gigs like that make you appreciate playing Wembley!'

Ironically, having repeated the miracle of *Pyromania*, by the end of 1988 as they settled down to a well-earned rest, Def Leppard found themselves back in the same predicament that the whole *Hysteria* phenomenon had begun with. How do you follow that? It was a question that exercised the collective brain, Joe understanding the difficulties only too clearly.

'Where do you go from stadiums? That's why we have managers. We have opinions but we don't have our finger on the pulse like they do. We're too busy, you can't be a master of all trades. When does a spectacle become untoppable? Satellite gigs? Hologram gigs? It's the same with the albums. The first album – I know it's a pile of shit – but it only took us three weeks to record and *High'n'Dry* only took three months. With *Pyromania* and *Hysteria*, we wanted to do something nobody had ever done before. On the next album, we don't wanna do that again. There comes a time when carrying the weight of experimentation on your shoulders gets a bit heavy. Maybe we just wanna do an album which says bollocks to all that. It might not kick any doors down, but who cares? We want to put an LP out in 1989 . . . we've spent three years with Mutt and learned a lot, but sooner or later, Grasshopper has to leave the temple and make his own way in the world. I'm not sure we'll even get to make that record yet, but if we do, we'll not be using Mutt. We also really want to release something that's not the official follow-up to *Hysteria*. It'll just be an odds and sods, penthouse tapes sort of thing, a few B-sides, a ton of new stuff and some stuff that's been recorded but not used yet.'

History proved that a 1989 release was hopelessly, wildlessly optimistic, but they did get set to begin work in March of that year. Having become the first band to sell seven million albums plus, back to back, there was no reason to quit, every reason to keep going. Joe pointed out on the release of *Hysteria* that 'most people in bands have got families and maybe that's the reason we have the success we have; nobody's married or got kids. There's enough kids without me bringing another one into the world. I don't want a kid – the band's too much of a bloody baby'. Touring the world had only strengthened the bond between the individuals and their loyalty to the Def Leppard cause. Joe summed it up by asking 'you know when you have a baby and it might be as ugly as shit, but you love it all the same? This band's our baby. And we still get on after seven years, five of them spent living out of each other's suitcases. We're each other's closest friends.' Those friendships would soon be put to the ultimate test.

9

THE LAST TIME

Without having dominated the front pages of the popular press, without carefully preening an image as devil-worshippers, without courting controversy, Def Leppard completed the *Hysteria* world tour as perhaps the biggest band in the world, eclipsing the popularity of the likes of U2 and Guns N'Roses. Instead of wasting energy on a public persona, all their time had been channelled into making the best possible records. It was a policy that had clearly paid handsome dividends. Nevertheless, there was more to Def Leppard's inexorable rise to prominence than mere songwriting proficiency.

Timing is of vital importance in the career of a band, especially if it wishes to rise above its contemporaries. The 1980s were a strikingly different time from any of the previous rock'n'roll decades, for the music no longer set the cultural agenda in the way that it had and was now seemingly relegated to reflecting society's mood. Though some shows such as Amnesty International's Conspiracy of Hope indicated that there were young fans willing to become politically engaged, the prevailing atmosphere was one of good times, parties, money and fun. Life was all about fast cars and great CD sound.

Perhaps the eighties love affair with technology came about because it was relatively benign – computerization was not yet requiring the massive job cuts that have been a feature of the nineties. The advance of technology seemed to be something to welcome, progress that would only change things for the better. Take

Leppard's field, the music industry. Improved studio facilities enabled producers and engineers to take a quantum leap forward, producing records the sound quality of which far outstripped anything that we'd ever thought possible. For a time, producers such as Mutt Lange, Bruce Fairbairn and Trevor Horn became as famous as their clients, such was the impact they had on the way we listened to music. Hand in hand with the development of the studio came the invention of digital recording and the compact disc, probably the most significant innovation in the last twenty-five years of musical history. With groups spending hundreds of thousands of pounds on their albums, working on them to get the clearest, crispest sound, they wanted them to be heard to best advantage. Cheap vinyl with its inherent problems of durability and quality was not good enough while cassettes were simply useless. The introduction of the CD was perfectly timed for artists who used the studio as another instrument.

By the same token, once you'd invested in a CD player, you wanted to get hold of some discs that showed your system off to its best advantage, something that sounded like 'Star Wars for the ears', a disc that would make full use of its capacity to amaze. Def Leppard's *Pyromania* was one of the first albums that could do that, *Hysteria* the album that took the concept still further. The CD age was made for Def Leppard just as they were made for the CD age. In the eighties, fewer people wanted music that made them feel, they just wanted tunes they could enjoy, that they could sing along with or dance to. Def Leppard with their minimal interest in the lyrics provided a goodtime soundtrack for an orgy of mindless materialism. Subconsciously too, the undemanding nature of Leppard's music suggested that technology would be similarly undemanding, for the two were indivisible – Leppard were technology, technology was represented by Leppard. Leppard were easy to listen to, they were bright and shiny, they were friendly, they were cuddly, so technology must therefore be the same.

Of course, Leppard were simply using the technology to make the music they enjoyed, fairly traditional rock in a modern setting. Other artists used it in a startlingly different way, illustrating the chaos or the coldness that change might provoke – New Order for instance or, later on, Ministry and Nine Inch Nails, while U2 also started to use the cutting edge of computerization to show a world torn apart by confusion. That kind of brutality, also exemplified by the burgeoning success of thrash metal, was not acceptable on a mainstream level in the 1980s when things seemed a lot more optimistic, especially if you had money. Joe made the point that 'thrash metal is a load of shit. There's no melody, no musicianship. The best guitar solos in the world are the ones you can sing – like the intro to "All the young dudes". I can't deal with stuff where you can't hear what the guy's singing. I can't hear many good songs coming out of thrash metal. It's not a music, it's an attitude, a way of life, a fashion. It's a pair of platform boots. I'd rather be a pair of straight-legged 501s.'

Ironically in the era of conspicuous consumption, it was a decade of anti-stars. The figureheads of the age were Bruce Springsteen and Bono, not obvious sex symbols nor men who luxuriated in their success or their wealth but who were apparently embarrassed by it. For those on the sidelines who were happily amassing a sizeable wad, this attitude was bizarre to say the least. They were only too glad to flaunt their GTIs or their Porsches, flash their Rolexes at passers-by and order another round of drinks. The cry of 'loadsamoney' summed up the age when people weren't really bothered by a social conscience, whatever Live Aid might have suggested, when the rate of tax was all that counted. Def Leppard were manna from heaven, a band who knew how to have a good time, who enjoyed being rich and made the most of their success. While members of Greenpeace took Michael Stipe as a hero, members of the yuppie culture took Leppard as theirs. They came to represent a way of life, though not necessarily one they would have fully endorsed.

That was not Leppard's only gift of course, for many who despised yuppiedom saw much to enjoy in the hard rocking tunefulness of 'Animal' or 'Photograph'. In essence, they provided a mindless, sugary antidote to the political polemic of Sting or Peter Gabriel, they were a guilty indulgence, all the more thrilling for it. At the same time, they did share common ground with Gabriel, Jim Kerr, Bruce or Bono, for this was also the time of 'good bloke' rock when bands were not populated with stars but with ordinary down to earth guys. Def Leppard was not filled with egocentric idiots, but a bunch of lads who you'd be happy to have a pint with at your local. Elliott remarked that 'A lot of people use the fact that they're famous as an excuse to act like a dickhead, but we don't bother with that nonsense.' At a time when Live Aid had made us all feel guilty about our comforts, someone like Joe Elliott could make you feel that you could do well for yourself and still be a decent guy. The gulf between them and their audience was never huge and that enabled them to win fans among the more serious rock supporters who had no time for a smartarse.

For a period of six years, Def Leppard had managed to pull off the considerable trick of being all things to all people, as good a way of guaranteeing multi-platinum sales as any. If they were starting to feel that sales figures were not the be-all and end-all of life, there was still no real motivation for changing their way of operating. People liked to buy their records, so they must have been giving them what they wanted. This was no time to disappoint them and so when, in the summer of 1989, they again got down to work in earnest, there seemed no need to try, for not only had Leppard done well but their contemporaries, Bon Jovi, had released *New Jersey* to enormous success.

The basic idea behind the new album was to find a happy medium between the polish of *Hysteria* and the aggression of *Pyromania*, there being a collective feeling that perhaps they'd taken too much notice of MTV's value to them and had sacrificed some of their musical muscle in the search for hit singles. They also wanted to work more quickly, for sound financial as well as musical reasons, even if Joe's suggestion that they might be able to release a record in 1989 was never likely to come to fruition. Things started out pretty well, writing sessions progressing at breakneck pace as Joe recalled: 'We wrote seven songs for the record in a week, it was a laugh, we were on a roll and it came out happy.' The caveat to that statement was that it was the last fun they'd have on the project.

Steve Clark was becoming more and more of a problem with every passing week, his descent into alcoholism more or less complete while his ability, even his desire, to recover seemed to diminish. As the band worked on through 1989 and into the new year, his very presence was having a hopelessly disruptive effect on progress. Things were awkward enough anyway since Mutt Lange was producing *Waking up the neighbours* for Bryan Adams, and Leppard were once again trying to produce themselves along with engineer Mike Shipley. In such unfamiliar conditions, the last thing they needed were problems with Clark which were every bit as significant as those which had lead them to fire Pete Willis during the recording of *Pyromania* in 1982. Joe summed up the situation: 'We couldn't get any work done. We were a five-piece operating as a four-piece and we had a moral dilemma about the whole thing. It was "we should be a band but instead it's Us and Him and Him isn't contributing because he's a complete and severe alcoholic who's killing himself".' An indication of their plight was the realization that six months of recording had yielded a mere two pieces of useable music – Phil's guitar solos on 'Tear it down' and 'Tonight'. If Leppard were the ultimate careerists that they are often painted as, Clark would have been quietly dumped in 1989 and a replacement sought. Where Willis had been obnoxious though, Clark was helpless and the band naturally wanted to help save their friend from himself. It was a long, painful process as Joe recalled. 'Since the "Hysteria" tour finished in October '88, Steve'd been in and out of rehab six times at least.'

Things seemed to have come to a head in December 1989 when they were taking a break from the album. Clark was found in Minnesota, comatose in a gutter and was, as is customary there in such cases, committed to a psychiatric hospital for observation. Once again, the incredible facts of the matter are burned on Elliott's memory. 'They told us the alcohol level in his blood was 0.59 when they found him. That didn't mean anything to us until they explained that a level of 0.41 had killed John Bonham.'

The psychiatric hospital only highlighted how desperate things had become. Joe visited his friend there: 'There were people scratching the walls and standing on one leg reciting the Lord's Prayer backwards. He didn't belong there, but he needed help from somewhere.' The doctors felt that Clark was simply ignoring the problem. The best medicine would be to confront him with the effects of his drinking, the impact he was having on the lives of his closest friends. He asked Elliott, Savage, Lange and Burnstein to write letters to Clark and then read them to him in a closed session. 'It was the most nerve-wracking thing I've ever had to do,' admitted Joe. 'It was awful. We'd lost him by then. Mutt saw him and said he'd got a dead man's skin and he was right. It was like orange peel, there was nothing in his eyes, he looked like he was dead already.'

Rick Savage felt similarly powerless to help and could only watch in horror as Clark's mental state deteriorated. 'Steve started to hate all the things that he'd loved in the past because he thought they trapped him. It was him that got us on stage in the first place right at the start. He loved the road but when we started to get ready for the big American tour for *Hysteria*, he actually tried to smash his hand so that he wouldn't be able to come. It drove us to desperation – he was such a nice person that you naturally try to protect him, look after him. It's only now that I realize how much time and effort we spent trying to care for him. We were like co-dependents. You have no other life apart from that.'

The only solution seemed to be work. Accepting that there would be another mighty gap between releases, Leppard settled on a more relaxed schedule, assisted by the fact that they'd settled down to work in Joe's home studio, a decision that also had much to do with the escalating cost of the record. That was one aspect of *Hysteria* that they did not wish to emulate. Joe joked with *Hot Press* that 'Aye lad, tha can tek the boy out of Sheffield, but tha can't tek Sheffield out of the boy! I put the studio in because I didn't want to spend two million quid making a record! Seriously, I am aware of things, I still look for the best price. I can't help it, I was born to very proud but average earning parents. I've always been conscious of not wasting money . . . we'd hear that Queen had a party with women swinging from chandeliers, serving champagne out of their bras and go "Wow! Great!" and then find it cost £120,000 and think, "hang on, that's eighteen grand each. I'd rather take it home and have a few pints". We'd only do that if someone else paid – tight-fisted bastards from Hell that we are!'

Joe felt that his tight control of the purse strings explained his refusal to get sucked into the drug culture. 'I'm materialistic which is why I never got hooked – I could never see the point of spending enough to stick coke up my nose that'd be gone in fifteen seconds when I could spend the same amount on ten CDs. The money I'd waste on drugs, I'd rather use to fly home to see Sheffield United, buy a load of CDs or some hi-fi. I don't wanna waste £300 on something that's gone in an hour; it's a waste of money and it's stupid. I'm not gonna die at thirty-five because of a dumb smack habit and I'm not gonna be skint at fifty either. Everything ends but I'm determined I'll be alright when it does.' Elliott was also blessed with a personality that was fairly equable, able to take a balanced view of things and to enjoy his success without wanting any stereotypical excess. Steve Clark was not so lucky.

It was important that, with Clark in such a state, sessions were not subject to the added stress of an over-stretched budget. Clark was not the only one able to take advantage of the new regime – Phil took three months off at the start of 1990 when his son Rory was born and, on his return, Joe jetted off for a break in Lanzarote. Phil felt that the time apart 'helped us be objective about each other's work'. Joe concurred, adding 'we just can't record quickly. Working at home, the environment helped. We had better security over the tapes, there was no pressure over time because studio time is so expensive. This time, if I couldn't sing on a given day, it just meant we finished a day later. No problem. To keep things moving, we recorded in split shifts – Phil did guitars eleven 'til six, I'd sing seven 'til midnight and if I knew I was having a bad time, Phil'd carry on playing.'

Those split shifts came in in 1991, for by then, Phil had twice as much work to do. Though Steve had returned to London from Minnesota, things were not improving. Because Steve wanted to keep his problem from his family, Joe went with him to his AA meetings, attempting to humiliate him into seeing his addiction in front of similar addicts, but to no avail. Joe recalled:

'He used to go to Alcoholics Anonymous meetings but he never believed he had a problem, that was the thing. He'd have a month or so in rehab, then he'd check out and go straight to the pub. To me, that's a guy that wants to die. I think he was just destined to destroy himself. It wasn't something that happened in the last few years, he'd been drinking heavily since I'd known him, puking blood back in '78. He was the best kept secret in rock'n'roll. Alcoholism is an illness and with all the will in the world, Steve couldn't stop. The lifestyle didn't help either. He'd

121

come round to the house and we'd hide the booze – he might have been off it for a couple of weeks – and he'd start asking why we'd hidden it and go all funny.'

The whole album was spinning further out of control and in September 1990, Steve was sent on a sabbatical by the rest of the group. Joe explained that 'We didn't fire him, we told him to sort himself out over six months – we couldn't deal with him being around in that state and we thought the best thing was to give him space. You're supposed to be an expert at handling it but you're not. Maybe in hindsight we should have spent more time with him, but you can't be your brother's keeper.' Not wishing to put an end to his career in the way they had with Willis, feeling that perhaps Def Leppard was Clark's only lifeline, all that kept him going, their reaction was a noble one. The sad truth was that Clark was an addict and far more medically and psychologically qualified and experienced professionals than four guys from a rock'n'roll band are constantly faced with failure as they try to break someone's habit. The band may still harbour feelings of guilt over the way they treated Clark, may feel there were things they could and should have done, but in truth they have no reason to reproach themselves. They did the very best they could under the circumstances and it just was not enough. Maybe nothing ever would have been.

On the morning of 8 January 1991, Steve Clark was found dead in his Chelsea flat. The coroner's report a month later stated that death had occurred because of a respiratory failure, resulting from excessive quantities of alcohol mixed with painkillers and anti-depressant drugs. Phrases like 'a shattering blow' tend to be trotted out at times like these, but no words can do justice to such traumatic news, even if it wasn't entirely unexpected as Rick Savage pointed out: 'Joe said to me sometime afterwards that it was almost like having an elderly relative that you know is going to die some time, but you don't think it's going to be today.' Joe made a statement on behalf of the band that summed up their feelings. 'Steve was a really quiet, shy, humble, nice, gentle sort of bloke. On stage, he was the business, very visual and very energetic, a great person to be alongside. Steve was a very creative person, the master of riffs, and wrote some of the best we've ever done. We'll definitely miss his creative input. It was a pleasure to know him for thirteen years and I'll miss him like a brother.'

Had Clark lived, then Leppard would almost certainly have had to get rid of him anyway, for he wasn't getting any better. Joe admitted as much, saying 'sooner or later we would have got to the stage where we would have had to decide "can we risk taking him on tour with us?" and I'd like to say he would have been fine, but I can't. How he stayed alive as long as he did was a blessing. He thought he was invincible, that he could drink forever but it doesn't work like that'. The comparisons with Pete Willis were inevitable, but no less painful for that. The question that constantly recurred was should Clark have been sacked years ago; would that have been the shock to the system that he needed or would it have merely escalated his decline? It was an insoluble question. Joe was understandably uncertain, saying 'I'm glad that Willis is alive and we get on okay. Ten years after the event, whenever I see him and he's on the wagon, he's fine. I'd much rather it be that way, there be a certain animosity between us but him alive than us love a guy who's dead. It was such a waste. So many people think that when you turn thirty, life's over – you die at thirty and life ain't even started'.

Phil Collen was deeply hurt by the loss of his close friend and playing partner, but like Joe, he was philosophical enough to realize that, given Steve's personality, it was sadly inevitable that things would end this way: 'He was alright on tour because your whole life is set out for you but as soon as he had time to sit down and think, he worried and worried and worried. The only escape was to hit the bottle. He was an alcoholic and it was horrible to see because it was my mate who was shaking and going "Fuck, I want to stop but I can't". I picked him up, carried him out of places and did all that stuff but you can only do so much. He kept trying but it went against him.'

The only consolation to be drawn from Clark's trials and eventual death was that he gave out a warning that was heeded by another member of the band who was in similar trouble. Rick Allen had long been thought of as fully recovered from his car accident, but beneath the surface, he was still trying to adapt to what had happened to him and its implications.

'I never went through any psychological rehabilitation after the accident. I just thought I could do it all on my own. I didn't realize until later on that I could have done with outside help. I never really gave myself time to get to know myself again. I was drinking, I'd got a gut and it was starting to show on my face. When we finally got a break in 1989, I spent some time trying to put all that right which was really important for me. I broke up with Miriam, my girlfriend of seven years, met up with an old girlfriend from 1980 and got married. I realized that the last thing I wanted to do was what Steve had done. I realized that everything in my life doesn't revolve around Def Leppard! I don't have anything to prove. But before that, when I tried to talk to Steve, when I tried to get him to see what was happening to him, he'd just come back at me with "what about your problems?" I couldn't get through that barrier, couldn't conquer my own troubles at that time.'

Just as they'd sought solace in their work when Rick lay in his hospital bed six years earlier, now they tried to do the same in the wake of Steve's death. Returning to Joe's Dublin home, they worked solidly for two months, but to no avail, Joe admitting that 'there was no soul in it'. As with *Hysteria*, the entire sessions were scrapped and work began afresh. This time, they really did want to put the record together quickly, not least because it was now almost four years since the release of *Hysteria*. However, Phil described other considerations that pushed them on: 'We recorded it again really quickly so we wouldn't have it hanging over us. We didn't want to dwell on it or get depressed by it. Making that record was really strange, we knew that we had this sound and that we were expected to do certain things. The sound got played out by other people and we were left wondering what the fuck to do next. We knew we had to write some stronger songs and change direction.'

Unfortunately, the band were so drained by their experiences with Clark that they were bereft of any fresh inspiration. Rick Allen admitted that 'I think we were going through the motions a bit, more concerned with Steve than anything else. We were on auto-pilot, making a record for the sake of it.' Joe agreed, adding 'we spent two years being miserable, but while we were recording it, we never thought we should change the sound of those original songs.' So, out of the most miserable period of their collective life came a record that was relentlessly upbeat, a record that seemed to shun any contact with the real world or with the real, raw emotions that they'd lived with.

They would have been much better advised to give free rein to their anguish. Having a five year gap between albums is not only costly, it's a high-risk strategy too. Fashion aside, there is no more ephemeral industry than popular music, nothing that moves with such bewildering pace. It was testimony to their creation that the sound they pioneered with *Pyromania* was still sufficiently popular in 1987 to turn *Hysteria* into an even bigger seller. Sadly, by 1992, the wheel had turned and misery was in vogue courtesy of Nirvana and the whole Seattle scene, while U2 had now become satirical industrial noiseniks courtesy of *Achtung Baby*. Alternative music had hit the mainstream with a vengeance and although *Adrenalize* sold in Leppard's customary humungous quantities, the album seemed woefully out of date and Leppard a band teetering on the brink of obsolescence. They knew it, though they tried to put a brave face on things, Joe saying 'it's more in your face, things are hitting you where they should. I honestly think that in five years' time, I'm going to think that *Adrenalize* is the best of the first five albums we did regardless of what comes over the next five years. We had more control over it and we got it exactly as we wanted it'.

Without Mutt Lange, the method of recording was appreciably different, though the results were strikingly similar to *Hysteria*, even if the sound was generally a little tougher. There were clear signs that the band were deliberately moving towards the heavier end of the spectrum, not in noise terms, but in the atmospheric and emotional tenor of some of the tracks. There was a Zeppelinesque emotional bottom to songs such as 'White lightning' that were an obvious departure for them and this mature work was clearly a pointer for the future. Ironically, Mutt Lange had attempted to veto its inclusion as Joe explained. 'We wanted the performances to be raunchier, the bollocks of *Pyromania* coupled with the songwriting capability of the last one. Initially we were trying to second guess Mutt but any time we got desperately stuck, we phoned him up in his capacity as Executive Producer and he'd make suggestions. I reckon we spoke thirty or forty times but most of the time we just got on with it. He wanted the optimistic stuff to go on the album, he was freaked out by "White lightning" which was mild as fuck.'

'White lightning' was the obvious centrepiece of *Adrenalize*, perhaps its saving grace. Joe described it as being 'about anyone that's gone down that avenue of self-destruction, be it Jim Morrison, Janis Joplin, Bon Scott, Steve Clark or someone on a bench outside McDonald's in Milton Keynes'. The eastern-influenced opening, similar in some ways to 'The cutter' by Echo and the Bunnymen, was a potent introduction to a song about addicts and addiction, the inability to break free of the shackles of a habit. Phil Collen was particularly outstanding on this song, while the anguished 'coming to claim you' section was incredibly strong. In all, it was a piece with real clout, something of which they could be proud and which Clark himself would have loved to have played on. Ironically it was Steve himself who had first pushed the band in this direction with 'Gods of war' on *Hysteria*. Sadly, it took his death to encourage them to go further down that road.

It was the only real evidence that Def Leppard might leave their own past behind them. *Adrenalize* was a rollicking rock'n'roll record with no pretensions to be anything else. By 1992, that wasn't really enough and the band that had prided itself on leading the field had finally missed a trick as their great rivals Bon Jovi had already seen which way the wind was blowing and were recording *Keep the faith*, a significant change of pace for them. Phil Collen spoke of the competition, pointing out that 'we're very competitive – *Adrenalize* isn't going to get played just against Bon Jovi or Guns N'Roses, but against Janet Jackson'. That was perfectly true, and in that company it performed exceptionally, topping the UK chart on release and spending five weeks at number one in the States. Artistically though, Leppard's standards had slipped for they were peddling music that had really had its final fling. Joe admitted as much, saying that 'it should have been out in 1990 – when it came out it should have sounded more like *Retro Active* or *Slang* but we spent half our time with Steve and our heart wasn't in it. It was a fucking horrible time'.

As has been pointed out, in spite of the ordeal, the music sounded as happy as any they'd produced. 'Let's get rocked' was as daft a song as you could find, in the same vein as 'Rocket', its use of effects both clever and amusing. Ironically though, after years of being too young to be a lecher, Joe's imploring 'S'pose a rock's out of the question?' was a double entendre that needed a younger man, though it remained endearingly silly. 'Heaven is' followed it up strongly, a nice tune, lashings of backing vocals and some of Brian May's stylized guitar explosions from Collen. It's sunny sound was infectious and it was difficult not to smile your way through it.

The Queen motif continued into 'Tonight', though it inevitably lacked Freddie Mercury's charismatic delivery and Queen's character. Nevertheless, it was not so overwrought as their earlier ballads and a real emotional quality was starting to emerge. The same was true of 'Have you ever needed someone so bad?', which was Joe's own *tour de force*, proof of just how far his voice had improved since 1979. An expert at playing the unrequited, lovelorn soul, this was classic 'lighters in the air' material, perfect for the concert hall. Strangely, it was Leppard's preoccupation with love songs of all shades that had been their greatest virtue on a commercial level. Savage accepting that 'we do look for the commercial aspect while keeping the power – it's a fine line'. Lyrically unimportant, it wasn't so much what they said, but the way that they said it, rockers and ballads alike building steadily to a crescendo before the final moment of release in a glorious chorus.

'Make love like a man' was a case in point, a rougher track but with a sturdy chorus and a memorable melody. 'Stand up (kick love into action)' was the band at their seductive best, a lush opening, decorous guitar and throaty vocals combining supremely well. The other three tracks, 'Personal property', 'I wanna touch you' and 'Tear it down' were standard rock'n'roll, songs that could have been on *Hysteria* but played with greater intent.

Adrenalize was a solid enough record, but ultimately rather characterless, the production this time not having the sheer scale to paper over the cracks. Lyrically, it was clear that the band had to move on, but it was a challenge that seemingly bewildered them. Joe argued that 'we like varying the sounds within songs, it's less tiring on the listeners' ears, subconsciously it makes it more appealing to people. We're really into metering and phrasing which is more important in rock'n'roll than actual lyrical content.' Speaking to *Q*, Joe took the prize for the most stupid attempt ever to justify their inane lyrics: 'The Brazilian rainforests and ozone layer are fine for some people but we'd rather help save them by giving them money so we can just make rock music. It might appear that a Def Leppard album isn't going to save the rainforest but it might, at the end of the day, if we cheer one person up enough to go and do something environmentally aware and do it while they're listening to us on their Walkman.'

In the face of such banality, it's no surprise that many dismissed Def Leppard as a wild anachronism, now thoroughly past their sell-by date. Yet Joe still complained that 'nobody takes what we do seriously. People who get credit for being innovative like the Thompson Twins, Jesus Jones, Blur and EMF don't sell jackshit compared to us. We're touching more people so it has to be better as far as I'm concerned . . . the only people who notice are record buyers. They're the most important people, but it does make you wonder.' Despite Joe's reservations, the album received some of the best reviews of their career. *Rolling Stone* called Leppard 'one of the catchiest bands in rock'n'roll, intensely tuneful, unrepentantly frivolous'. Paul Elliott gave them nine out of ten in *Vox*, and noted that *Adrenalize* was 'sure to be a definitive multi-million seller . . . for Collen in particular, it's a triumph. Less of Lange's studio trickery, more of a straightforward hard rock record. "Stand up" is the perfect pop metal single. There's little wonder that Jimmy Page and David Coverdale's *Legends* album has been shelved until October . . . *Adrenalize* will be *the* rock album of the summer'. Fiona Looney in *Hot Press* marked them equally well, ten out of twelve, and endorsed the group's attitude in gushing terms: 'A terrace-friendly record of excitement, energy, optimism, elation and adrenaline . . . the Leps rely almost exclusively on good old-fashioned foot-stomping, air-punching, roaring rock'n'roll . . . easy mind-numbing fare that appeals to the heart and the feet without taxing the head, but surely that's what rock'n'roll should be and what it was before it was hijacked by whingers like Bob Dylan.' Only Phil Sutcliffe in *Q* wondered how they had come through their personal tragedies so unscathed: 'For better or worse, they seem to have come through the long process of emotional turmoil and relentlessly professional self-criticism with exactly the album everyone was expecting . . . *Adrenalize* adds up to efficiency . . . if it sounds safe, it also sounds like another commercial monster.'

The problem was that at this stage of their career, was safe but sure really good enough? Shouldn't Leppard be extending themselves further, moving in circles where they weren't so convinced of their ability? In short, wasn't it time to take a chance or two? After all, they scarcely needed the money any longer. There was evidence that this was exercising their minds rather more, but it was a problem that had to be shelved. The latest tour was looming, bringing with it a huge problem. How did they replace Steve Clark?

Phil Collen didn't even want to try: 'Steve was my best friend and the thought of replacing him was crap – you don't go out and get a new brother. It took me a year to come to terms with the fact that we needed another guitarist.' Eventually though, Phil accepted that it would be impossible for Leppard to take to the stage as a four-piece band and recreate their album performances in anything approaching meaningful fashion. The die was cast and, after intensive auditions, Vivian Campbell got the job. Born in Northern Ireland and a seasoned hard rock guitarist, having had spells with Sweet Savage, Dio and Whitesnake among others, Campbell's style fitted in well alongside Collen and the two were swift to develop a good working relationship. Unfortunately, it didn't develop quickly enough to prevent one of his earliest gigs with the band turning into a disaster. In April 1992, they played Wembley Stadium as part of the Freddie Mercury tribute concert, a gig that was being broadcast to the world. The band were dreadful, Rick's drum kit having got lost beforehand delaying their appearance and then their sound apparently coming from the bottom of a swamp.

The accompanying tour, in the round again, was enormously successful, propelling *Adrenalize* towards sales that even rivalled those of *Hysteria*, though *Melody Maker*'s John Selzer was unimpressed by their Earl's Court performance calling them 'a lifeline for the comatose – Mills & Boon novels, Australian soap drama and

Def Leppard songs . . . it was zombiefied, for disenfranchized consumers of the dream'. The whirl of touring activity continued well into 1993, the band finally enjoying the shows once more now that the atmosphere in the band had improved with Campbell's addition. Elliott commented memorably that 'it's not a ball and chain any more, you don't wake up on tour any more wondering if the guy in the next room is going to be dead.'

There was even time to piece together the ragbag of B-sides and rarities that Joe had spoken about five years previously. In October 1993, *Retro active* came out, indicating that Leppard were a band that were starting to reassess their place in the scheme of things, *Q*'s Valerie Potter writing that the album was a 'pleasantly patterned patchwork that is, in many ways, preferable to their more contrived, overtly commercial releases'. This new looseness, the product of the relaxed state of mind that accompanies any such compilation, was an inspiration for the future, the record itself having much to commend it. There were epic Zeppelin influences on 'Desert song', the Queen-style cover of the Sweet's 'Action', the newly minted delicacy of touch on the mega-ballad 'Miss you in a heartbeat', the Irish folk-rock of the brooding 'From the inside', the peerless lovers' rock of 'Two steps behind' and the boisterous bouncy pop of 'I wanna be your hero'. It was obvious that this was a group finally heading into its full maturity, ready perhaps to do its best work and with a steady grasp of a diverse range of music.

Another stopgap album in 1995, the obligatory greatest hits set, *Vault*, not only offered a breathing space to enable them to complete their next record without such an unseemly gap between releases, but it provided a punctuation mark, adding further fuel to the rumours that Def Leppard were ready to put the first phase of their career to bed and emerge again with something rather different.

10

TIME FOR A CHANGE?

They were lucky to get away with it. *Adrenalize* succeeded thanks to a loyal fan base and a huge promotional budget, much of which was consumed by the video for 'Let's get rocked' which kick-started the album across America. Even then, there was no disguising that this was yesterday's music, a fact that Leppard were willing to own up to, Savage suggesting that 'it was obvious to us that we really wanted a break from the way we'd always recorded, we wanted a different sound'.

Whether you're a fan or not, it's impossible not to concede that Nirvana and U2 radically reshaped mainstream music at the beginning of this decade. U2's particular brand of angst had always been popular, but it was couched in such musical terms as to remain uplifting, ultimately optimistic. With *Achtung Baby* that was behind them for though their lyrical and spiritual preoccupations were broadly similar, their vocabulary was overhauled, culminating in a darker, claustrophobic noise. 'The fly' was not from the same whistle-friendly stable as 'I still haven't found what I'm looking for', but the public still lapped it up. No-one would call 'Smells like teen spirit' a candidate for a Michael Bolton record, but its sales surpassed even his. The shiny, happy audience of the 1980s, fans who were perfect for Leppard's sunny, sugary pop-rock were mutating into the Generation X crowd. Grunge reflected their take on a world that was changing too fast, a world that offered little, where the promised future for those who worked hard was evaporating before their eyes.

The benign technology that had given us the CD was now consuming the anticipated job for life and leaving the rock audience – who as youngsters were off into the workplace – dazed and confused. Phil Collen noted that 'in the eighties, it was the social climate that demanded our style of music. Everything was different, everyone had money, that was the impression. But we were looked on as the McDonalds of rock music. It was partly because the lyrics were so shallow, partly because we sounded so polished. In the nineties, misery became cool and when we were touring *Adrenalize*, we just didn't fit. We had to put things right, make our lyrics stronger especially.'

A regular criticism of Leppard – though paradoxically it's also a source of their strength – was their rigidity, their perceived lack of adaptability. The *Adrenalize* project confirmed that, for although Steve Clark died during its making, that did not deflect them from their chosen path of upbeat, raucous rock'n'roll. Similarly, their intricate way of working in the studio, their concentration on getting every final aspect of a song, its arrangement and its production, to their liking before allowing its release was a guarantee of a certain quality, but also militated against the songs sounding like anything but another Leppard product. Such attention to detail, such a quest for perfection meant that sacrifices had to be made along the way with some songs overworked to the point of exhaustion.

The buzzwords in the camp now were 'looser', 'relaxed', 'heavier'. How their meticulous preparation would stack up alongside these particular ambitions would decide how successful the reinvention of Def Leppard would be. Looking back at their canon, Collen felt that 'our previous albums were intelligent on a musical level but this time around we wanted to be freer. It was a reaction to recording separately under the microscope. It was fun, the guitars were generally one take, we didn't spend time getting sounds, all our effort went into the songs, not the production. We spent eighteen months on it, with a definite target in mind.'

One thing that helped this time around was the fact that a blueprint existed. Making *Pyromania* and *Hysteria*, Leppard had been attempting to freshly mint a sound that no-one had made in the past and as Joe pointed out 'we're prepared to go that extra yard. And sometimes you don't know where that extra yard is which is why it takes such a long time to get there'. Now, they were following in the footsteps of many other bands, taking inspiration from a wider range of music and knowing precisely what they were looking for. That immediately removed the pressure and turned recording into fun.

To maintain that lighter mood, they chose to rent a house in Marbella, where they would record from May 1994 onwards – apparently, the villa was used as the home of villain Ally Fraser in the second series of the TV comedy drama *Auf Wiedersehen, Pet*. The atmosphere was idyllic, Joe informing jealous reporters that 'if you weren't ready to work, you could just go and look out at the ocean, which was much better, much more inspiring, than the dungeons we usually record in'. Phil compared the whole experience with 'going on a school holiday, there was a new enthusiasm in Spain. It was almost like being in a new band, and the record reflected that. It's about us, not about production.'

The change in emphasis has proved to be a resounding success, if not the radical rebirth that advance publicity might have suggested. There are still elements of quintessential Leppard on show, but the changes that have taken place are not superficial. Determined to remain valid in a new decade, the reassessment that has taken place is similar to the way Genesis restructured their sound in 1981 with *Abacab*. Then, the traditional size of the sound was trimmed back, allowing songwriting rather than musical talent to shine through. Genesis brought in a new producer to help free themselves from habits and preconceptions. Leppard did the same, drafting in Pete Woodroffe as co-producer while Lange had little or no involvement, not even getting involved with the songwriting process. The accent is on strong songs and on strong characters; this is the heart of *Slang* and consequently the material ranks among the best they've yet produced.

Though they worked long and hard on the record – in Marbella from May until September 1994, two months more in Dublin, back to Spain until May 1995, then, following the promotional chores for *Vault*, two more months to finish off – there is no sense in which this is a laboured record. It has a livelier feel than any previous album, even though musically it's quite dark, the product of the obligatory harrowing times that accompanied it; Rick Savage lost his father while Phil continues to go through a divorce all the more traumatic because of the question of custody of his young son. Where before the band simply ignored life, now its vicissitudes are grist to the songwriting mill. Phil's 'Breathe a sigh' is a fine example of that, a yearning ballad that reflects on his loss. Musically, it's the most atypical song Leppard have ever recorded, lazy swingbeat pop that calls to mind Take That, though the idea of Leppard performing a syncopated dance routine on the world's concert stages remains an unlikely one. Collen accepted that 'if it's the best of a style, it has to be an influence, whether it's Nirvana or Boyz II Men.'

If you're going to steal, steal from the best has been a motto that has kept every decent rock'n'roll band in business since time immemorial. If Boyz II Men provided the platform for 'Breathe a sigh', Nirvana had more than a hand in 'Deliver me', one of the album's standout songs. Joe's voice was gruff, as though he'd taken on a nastier alter-ego. The lyric was harsh in the extreme, the song's protagonist shutting someone out for good, touching also on spiritual matters and a lack of faith, a subject that was to recur on the album.

In tone, the album was impressionistic, morose, devoid of the blatant love songs that had cropped up elsewhere. To reinforce the mood of change, even the sleeve artwork was modernized, replacing the dreadful artwork they'd persisted with through the rest of their career. This time, the cover betrayed a strong Indian influence as did some of the music. 'Turn to dust' was a case in point, a song that exploited Joe's expanding emotional range and the constantly improving partnership between Campbell and Collen, Allen noting that 'it was a group thing this time. When Viv came in, the whole thing became more of a team'.

In modern rock music, use of that eastern sound inevitably leads you to think either of the Beatles, particularly George Harrison, or Led Zeppelin, notably 'Kashmir'. There were traces of both on 'Turn to dust', while Rick added a modern dimension with his use of the shuffle beat so prevalent in the 'baggy' movement, personified by the Stone Roses and Happy Mondays.

Although it was Phil Collen who was the major writer on *Slang*, it was Allen who was pivotal in directing the sound: 'After the first two albums, the electronic kit was more convenient, partly because it was easier after I lost my arm, but also because of the kind of records we were making. As we changed tack, it seemed right to go back to the acoustic kit to get a more earthy sound. I also missed the physical side of hitting the drums. The sound just set the tone.' Collen agreed, saying 'we wanted Rick to use the acoustic kit that he still used at home and it sounds so much better on what we're trying to do now.' Listening to 'Turn to dust' and its predecessor, the album opener 'Truth?', the startling realization was that rather than listening for the production tricks, it was the band's own personality that was striking home. 'Truth?' for example featured heavily industrialized vocals that were somehow more humanly authentic than Joe's normal transatlantic drawl and it was lovely to hear real drums again. There was more interaction between the five members of Def Leppard on those two songs than on the previous two fully-fledged albums; they finally sounded as if they were playing together as a band in the studio.

'Slang' itself was the choice as lead-off single, and an interesting one at that. Joe felt that 'it's the only thing with a foot in the old camp, three minutes of pop about phone sex', but that was un-characteristically modest for though it was pop music, it was a long way from 'Let's get rocked'. From the same school as the rap-metal style of Terrorvision, Slang had an exuberance that one would have expected from a band making their first album, not one in its eighteenth year. A little disappointing that it was chosen as the first single when riskier choices existed, they can be forgiven for wanting to break in the old fans gently.

Those more traditional supporters could still find a lot to enjoy on *Slang* for they were clearly not to be alienated by it. Viv Campbell's 'Work it out' was tremendously catchy, an obvious hit single though in a different way to something like 'Animal'. The sound was truly thunderous, with Joe's restrained vocal only adding to the impact. 'All I want' used their trademark vocals, an inescapable, overwhelming sound, topped off by a fine closing guitar refrain from Collen.

Even so, they were clearly in the grip of change. Rick Savage felt that 'it wasn't so much a change as something we'd been wanting to do for a few years. It was easier to make *Slang* than a record that sounded like what we'd been doing for the last eight or ten years.' Phil was a little unsure of their ground before recording, worrying about the change in gear, but had to admit 'there's nothing wrong with it which is a surprise because we were afraid of it. If you stay with the same sound, you become like Wishbone Ash or something which is a shame.' Joe was adamant that they had to make this leap: 'It was a logical progression. We could have carried on, pretending to be the champions of teenage rock but as you get older, it becomes stupid. We'd made our trilogy of big production albums and during the *Adrenalize* tour, it was just so obvious that we wanted to do something different – it's not a dance floor production for sure!' The final four songs indicated that they were growing up as a band and touching on subjects that would have been taboo just a few years before.

'Gift of flesh' employed volume with intent rather than with bluster, another of Phil's songs that dwelt on the darker side of his psyche, juxtaposing a loss of faith with an almost Catholic dose of guilt, a recurrent theme on the swing laden 'Where does love go when it dies?' On 'Blood runs cold', the music was as chilling as the theme, a lyric that looked at the futility of suicide, perhaps inspired by Kurt Cobain and by the loss of Steve Clark whose addiction was tantamount to a death wish. With Savage having lost his father, the value of life could only have been brought home still further to the band, a message that was implicit in 'Blood runs cold'. 'Pearl of euphoria' was a fitting conclusion to what was becoming a very cathartic album. Joe felt that it 'was quite an inward looking song', the personal nature of it leading him to cloud its meaning in oblique references and impressionistic phrases. If it described his own state of mind, then Planet Elliott was not quite the happy go lucky place it often appeared, for the imagery was bleak, the addictive phrases reminiscent of 'White lightning' and the music doomladen. A potent end to Def Leppard's finest hour.

Reviews were mixed, *Q* suggesting that the changes were radical while *Vox* felt that nothing had altered. Probably the best summary came from *Metal Hammer*, which termed it 'their most diverse work so far. The band are tapping into different areas but rarely do you get the impression that a rock's out of the question!' At the time of writing, *Slang* has just hit the shops, so the public's verdict is not yet in. It will be interesting to see how many of their ardent supporters take the necessary leap of faith with the band.

Live dates will inevitably follow, the gigs showing an evolution equal to that on the album. Rick Allen suggests that 'the emphasis will be on us, not the set. It was getting to be too much', while born again rocker Joe Elliott sees it as 'us, a few lights and lots of Marshalls'. Early indications are that if the new album is as well received as they hope, Def Leppard could be touring the world for the next two years, bringing their own brand of rock'n'roll to a venue near you, wherever you are. When the dust settles, the process will start again for with *Slang*, Leppard have made it clear that they intend to remain valid for years to come. Just don't expect another new album this millennium.

11

ALL WE WANT IS EVERYTHING

Trying to sum up Def Leppard's career is a peculiarly difficult task. There are few, if any, bands that have been so deliberately and defiantly ambitious, so manic in their need to over achieve, so calculating in their game plan. As a bunch of teenagers in Sheffield, the music they loved united them as did a fierce compulsion to use it as a passport to a better life. Reviled by the critics for their fascination with commerce, they have gone on to write the rule book for making it big in the music industry.

Never impressed by bands who made great play of a terrible relationship with their employees, Leppard did their utmost to ingratiate themselves with Phonogram, working themselves into the ground in the process. No TV show, no interview, no meet and greet that might help advance their cause has ever been needlessly refused while their regard for and generosity towards the fans is legendary; Phil Collen is renowned for spending hours talking to them at gigs and hotels.

Yet Leppard have never been treated with much respect by the press, Collen admitting that 'we're as hip as piles!' Though they have their share of talented musicians, none of them would necessarily be at the forefront when it comes to selecting a band to play in the Rock'n'Roll Fantasy League. The consensus of opinion is that Leppard are made up of forthright, hardworking journeymen, an allegation which they do very little to dispel. Talking of the competition, Joe feels that 'Jagger's the best. The ultimate frontmen are those you can caricature in cartoons – Jagger, Steven Tyler, Rod Stewart, Bowie, Townshend, Meat Loaf, Alice Cooper. You couldn't really draw me but it doesn't seem to have hindered our success.' Such humility is one of the lessons learned early on following a meeting with one of the legends of the hard rock game as Joe recalls. 'When we first met Brian May, he came up and said "Hello, I'm Brian May from Queen." As if we didn't know, it's like the Queen introducing herself. We said "what a guy, down to earth, spot on". You make a mental note, you learn from other people.'

At the same time, Leppard have been protected from the vagaries of life by a breathtaking arrogance, an utter conviction that 'we're the best. In what we do, nobody can touch us'. Unfairly over the years, they've been portrayed as Mutt Lange's creation, casting Lange as Frankenstein to Leppard's monster. It's a long way from the truth. Before setting foot in the studio for *Pyromania*, Leppard were well aware that they wanted to break the mould of hard rock recordings. They had a very clear vision of what they wanted to do having spotted an area that no-one else was catering for and followed that vision to the hilt. Lange was crucial, but largely as an interpreter rather than an instigator. With the colossal dedication to the cause that has been at the heart of their armoury, they would not be diverted from their goal. The bile of British audiences was treated with something approaching contempt; Phonogram's anxiety over the gap between *High'n'dry* and *Pyromania* was dismissed; Allen's horrifying accident was overcome; Steve Clark's awful death was pushed aside. Nothing could deflect Def Leppard. Joe is perfectly correct in stating that 'one of the greatest qualities in this band is willpower, much more than talent. Some people won't sing a top C because it's hard, but I'll keep going until I get it right. If you practice long enough, you get there in the end. The word "can't" isn't in our vocabulary. We've got this reference point that says if you can have a one-armed drummer, you can do owt!'

Perhaps it's a reflection of our times that a band who think of themselves as honest craftsmen rather than multi-talented artists can become the biggest in the world, amassing album sales well in excess of forty million. In another age, maybe such a utilitarian combination as Def Leppard would not have earned a second glance. That might be the case but all that the band could do, can do, is their very best. In that, they have given an object lesson to any young group coming up behind them. Make the absolute most of your talents, use your intelligence to look for new angles, and success may yet be yours.

You can't think about Def Leppard without reflecting on the casualties. MSB were the first, Pete Willis the next, Rick Allen lived to tell the tale, Steve Clark tragically did not. In one way or another, all of those, bar Allen, lacked the almost psychotic devotion to the band that the rest demanded, though Clark was eventually in no fit state to commit himself to anything. Possibly the rest of the band didn't deal with the issues as sensitively as they could have, perhaps in Clark's case they were almost too supportive, but they've always lived by the maxim that the show must go on. That's not to say that they're brutal, for the friendship extended to Rick Allen was striking, but overall nothing is allowed to come between the group and their goal.

Operating within such a taut working environment is not likely to lead to an easy life, and sacrifices have had to be made along the way as Elliott recounts. 'You forsake being able to go to the pub with your mates, going to a football match if you have to rehearse. You forsake your girlfriend, you don't see your parents very often. But what you lose on the one hand you gain on the other, like the immense camaraderie on tour.' The shock of Clark's death has given them cause to rethink their priorities though as Allen points out 'we do take it all a lot more light-heartedly now. But we still want to be legendary. We want to get on the cover of a rock history book. How's that for cliché!'

In the end, that's what Def Leppard are about – setting the most unlikely target and then working towards it in the most blinkered of fashions. But they always seem to get there. Savage admits to the importance of the work ethic, saying 'we spend all our time just trying to stay ahead of the game. We don't stop and we don't look down.'

The final word goes to the garrulous Elliott, bringing the story full circle.

'In the winter of 1978, me and Pete Willis were walking home from the rehearsal room and we had enough money to buy one pint between us or take the bus home. We had a pint with two straws, huddled round a fire in a pub near Bramall Lane. We walked home past Sheffield City Hall where I found some chalk and wrote "Def Leppard will play here in 1980" on the wall. We sold it out in 1980 and thought we'd made it. Now, years later, there's always room for improvement; we don't want to go backwards like Uriah Heep or Wishbone Ash and keep on playing when nobody cares. We don't want to be a one-off. At home I've got a disc for *Pyromania* and *Hysteria* for the first septuple million back-to-back albums in history. We were the first to do that. That's one side. The other is that we've done two nights at Wembley Arena and two at the NEC but not five nights at Wembley Stadium where Guns N'Roses sold 450,000 tickets in one day. There's always more.'

UK DISCOGRAPHY

SINGLES
Getcha rocks off
January 1979
See notes

Wasted
November 1979
Chart: 61

Hello America
February 1980
Chart: 45

Let it go
August 1981
See notes

Bringin' on the heartbreak
November 1981
See notes

Photograph
January 1983
Chart: 66

Rock of ages
August 1983
Chart: 41

Too late for love
November 1983
See notes

Animal
July 1987
Chart: 6

Pour some sugar on me
September 1987
Chart: 18

Hysteria
November 1987
Chart: 26

Armageddon it
April 1988
Chart: 20

Love bites
July 1988
Chart: 11

Rocket
January 1989
See notes

Let's get rocked
March 1992
Chart: 2

Make love like a man
June 1992
Chart: 12

Have you ever needed someone so bad
September 1992
Chart: 16

Heaven is
January 1993
Chart: 13

Tonight
April 1993
Chart: 34

Two steps behind
September 1993
Chart: 32

Action
January 1994
Chart: 14

When love and hate collide
1995
Chart: 6

Slang
April 1996
Chart: 17

ALBUMS
ON THROUGH THE NIGHT
Rock brigade/Hello America/Sorrow is a woman/It could be you/
Satellite/When the walls came tumbling down/Wasted/Rocks off/It
don't matter/Answer to the master/Overture

March 1980
Chart: 15

HIGH'N'DRY

Let it go/Another hit and run/High'n'dry (Saturday night)/Bringin'
on the heartbreak/Switch 625/You got me runnin'/Lady strange/On
through the night/Mirror, mirror (Look into my eyes)/No no no
July 1981
Chart: 26

PYROMANIA

Rock! Rock! (Till You Drop)/Photograph/Stagefright/Too late for
love/Die hard the hunter/Foolin'/Rock of ages/Comin' under fire/
Action! not words/Billy's got a gun
February 1983
Chart: 18

HYSTERIA

Women/Rocket/Animal/Love bites/Pour some sugar on me/
Armageddon it/Gods of war/Don't shoot shotgun/Run riot/
Hysteria/Excitable/Love and affection
August 1987
Chart: 1

ADRENALIZE

Let's get rocked/Heaven is/Make love like a man/Tonight/White
lightning/Stand up (Kick love into motion)/Personal property/Have
you ever needed someone so bad/I wanna touch you/Tear it down
March 1992
Chart: 1

RETRO ACTIVE

Desert song/Fractured love/Action/Two steps behind (acoustic
version)/She's too tough/Miss you in a heartbeat/Only after dark/
Ride into the sun/From the inside/Ring of fire/I wanna be your hero/
Miss you in a heartbeat (electric version)/Two steps behind (electric
version)

October 1993
Chart: 6

VAULT
Pour some sugar on me/Photograph/Love bites/Let's get rocked/
Two steps behind/Animal/Heaven is/Rocket/When love and hate
collide/Action/Make love like a man/Armageddon it/Have you ever
needed someone so bad/Rock of ages/Hysteria/Bringin' on the
heartbreak
October 1995
Chart: 4

SLANG
Truth?/Turn to dust/All I want is everything/Work it out/Breathe a
sigh/Deliver me/Gift of flesh/Blood runs cold/Where does love go
when it dies/Pearl of euphoria
May 1996
Chart: 5

SOURCES

HOT PRESS
Live review, Cork Connolly Hall by Tony O'Donoghue, 26 August 1986.
Hysteria LP review by Jon de Leon, 10 September 1987.
'If I'd Spent Eighteen Months In Los Angeles' . . ., 24 September 1987.
Adrenalize LP review by Fiona Looney, 23 April 1992.
'I'm A Rocker' by George Byrne, 23 April 1992

MAKING MUSIC
'In Def There Is Life' by Andrea Thorn, May 1992.

MELODY MAKER
'Growing Up In Public' by Brian Harrigan, 10 January 1981.
Live review, Hammersmith Odeon by Steve Gett, 8 August 1981.
Live review, Marquee Club by Nick Kemp, 19 February 1983.
'Pyromaniacs!' by Frank Worrall, 2 April 1983.
'Til Deaf Do Us Part' by Derek Oliver, 10 December 1983.
Live review, Birmingham Odeon by Simon Scott, 17 December 1983.
Live review, Hammersmith Odeon by Chris Roberts, 19 September 1987.
'Travelling Band' by Carol Clerk, 9 April 1988.
Live review, Toulouse Grand Palais Des Sports by Carol Clerk,

8 April 1988.
Live review, Earls Court by John Selzer, 11 July 1992.
'Rebellious Jukebox' by Joe Elliott, 16 October 1993.

METAL HAMMER
Slang LP review by Dave Ling, June 1996.
'You Don't Wake Up On Tour . . .' by Jerry Ewing, June 1996.

NEW MUSICAL EXPRESS
'Are You Crap? Yeah, We Are' by Deanne Pearson, 29 September 1979.
'More Brutes & Loonies', 1 March 1980.
'We Wanted To Be The Biggest . . .' by Steven Wells, 21 January 1989.

Q
Hysteria LP review by Emily Fraser, October 1987.
'Loadsamoney' by Mat Snow, May 1988.
Adrenalize LP review by Phil Sutcliffe, May 1992.
'Life Is Sweet' by John Aizlewood, May 1992.
Retro Active LP review by Valerie Potter, December 1993.

RECORD MIRROR
'Armageddon Time' by Ian Dickson, 23 April 1988.
'Star Trekkin'' by Lisa Tilston, 30 July 1988.
'Blast Off' by Roger Morton.

SMASH HITS
'What A Bunch Of Weeds' by Silvia Patterson, 12 August 1987.
'Most Successful Rock Singer In The World' by Richard Lowe, 22 February 1989.

SOUNDS
'The New Wave Of British Heavy Metal' by Geoff Barton, 16 June 1979.
'Hello America' single review by Mick Middles, 23 February 1980.
'Def Or Glory?' by Geoff Barton, 1 March 1980.

On through the night LP review by Geoff Barton, 22 March 1980.
Live review, Newcastle by Ian Ravensdale, 26 April 1980.
'Def For Glory' by Pete Makowski, 4 July 1981.
High'n'dry LP review by Geoff Barton, 18 July 1981.
'The Luxury Of Real Fur' live review, Hammersmith Odeon by Philip Bell, 8 August 1981.
Pyromania LP review by Geoff Barton, 12 February 1983.
'It's Better To Burn Out Than Fade Away' by Geoff Barton, 5 March 1983.
'Spot Cash For Metal' by Garry Bushell, 6 August 1983.
'Will The Rollercoaster Red Carpet Ride Ever Stop' by Robbi Millar, 25 July 1987.
'Cat Scratch Fever', *Hysteria* LP review by Paul Elliott, 22 August 1987.
'Sugar On The Rocks', live review, Nottingham Royal Centre by Paul Elliott, 12 September 1987.
'Magic Roundabout' by Paul Elliott, 5 December 1987.
Live review, Wembley Arena by Mary Anne Hobbs, 23 April 1988.
'Once Bitten Twice Shy' by Mary Anne Hobbs, 2 July 1988.
'Bringing Up Baby' by Mat Snow, 18 February 1989.

VOX
Adrenalize LP review by Paul Elliott, May 1992